REPLY

OF THE

TRUSTEES OF UNION COLLEGE,

TO

CHARGES BROUGHT BEFORE THE ASSEMBLY OF NEW-YORK,

March 19, 1850; and before the

Senate, on the 12th of April, 1851,

By the Hon. J. W. BEEKMAN.

This reply was prepared and nearly all printed previous to the Meeting on the 1st of March, 1853, of the Commissioners appointed to examine and report on the charges against Union College and its officers, and would have been presented to them, had they allowed the College and its officers to be heard in their defence, previous to the majority sending in with their sanction to the Senate, the exparte statements of the accountant employed by them. The resolution appointing them, contemplated such a hearing of the parties accused; it was twice claimed by the trustees; it was repeatedly promised by the Rev. John N. Campbell, chairman of the commission, but was, notwithstanding, refused; and a mass of matter, of which the trustees and officers were wholly ignorant and which they never were allowed to examine, was sent forth to the world, to prejudice them and induce the worst impressions of their official conduct.

ALBANY:

CHARLES VAN BENTHUYSEN, PRINTER.

No. 407 Broadway.

1853.

REPLY

OF THE

TRUSTEES OF UNION COLLEGE,

TO

CHARGES BROUGHT BEFORE THE ASSEMBLY OF NEW-YORK,

March 19, 1850; and before the

Senate, on the 12th of April, 1851,

BY THE HON. J. W. BEEKMAN.

This reply was prepared and nearly all printed previous to the Meeting on the 1st of March, 1853, of the Commissioners appointed to examine and report on the charges against Union College and its officers, and would have been presented to them, had they allowed the College and its officers to be heard in their defence, previous to the majority sending in with their sanction to the Senate, the exparte statements of the accountant employed by them. The resolution appointing them, contemplated such a hearing of the parties accused; it was twice claimed by the trustees; it was repeatedly promised by the Rev. John N. Campbell, chairman of the commission, but was, notwithstanding, refused; and a mass of matter, of which the trustees and officers were wholly ignorant and which they never were allowed to examine, was sent forth to the world, to prejudice them and induce the worst impressions of their official conduct.

ALBANY:

CHARLES VAN BENTHUYSEN, PRINTER.

No. 407 Broadway.

1853.

THE TRUSTEES OF UNION COLLEGE,

To the commissioners appointed to examine the charges made by Senator Beekman.

UNION COLLEGE,
Schenectady, *July* 23, 1851.

GENTLEMEN,—The undersigned have been appointed by the Trustees of Union College to attend before you and assist in the investigation of charges which have been made and extensively circulated, and which are calculated to impair the confidence of the public in the institution, and to injuriously affect the reputation of its venerable and distinguished President. Believing, as the Board of Trustees do, that these charges have no foundation in truth, they are anxious that a speedy as well as full examination of the subject should be had. We therefore request that the earliest practicable day should be appointed by you to commence the investigation, and that all the investigating commissioners should attend thereon. We also desire to be informed of the time and place of meeting, and that the members of the Senate committee by whom the charges have been brought before the public, should also have notice, and that they be requested to furnish you with the evidence upon which their report was based, and the sources of information to which you are to apply for evidence in support of the charges contained in their report.

Permit us to suggest that if the convenience of the commissioners should render it necessary to carry on the investigation at any place other than the College, that such investigation may take place during the present vacation, as it will be necessary that several officers of the College should be present to give the requisite explanations of complicated accounts which have run through more than half a century, and such officers cannot be spared from their duties from the College during the collegiate terms, to attend the meeting of the commissioners at any other place without serious detriment to the institution.

We are with respect, yours, &c.,

R. H. WALWORTH.
R. M. BLATCHFORD.
A. HUNT.
B. R. WOOD.

Revd. Dr. John N. Campbell, Philo C. Fuller, L. S. Chatfield, Ph. Van Rensselaer, David Buel, Jun., Esqrs.

Commissioners.

Rev. Dr. Campbell's Letter.

Caldwell, Lake George,
August 1, 1851.

Rev. Dr. Nott,

Sir—The commission appointed by the Senate to examine into the affairs of Union College, and report upon the same to the next Legislature, have resolved to enter on the duty assigned them, by the examination of the account books and vouchers of the College.

Mr. Van Derheyden has been appointed the accountant of the commission, and is hereby authorized to receive said books and papers at the State Office in Albany. Be pleased to deliver them to him on his presentation of this order.

By order of the Commission.

Very respectfully,

J. N. CAMPBELL.

Rev. Dr. Nott's Answer.

Union College,
September 12, 1851.

Rev. and dear sir—I have delivered the books and papers, as desired, to Mr. Van Derheyden, who has just called for the same, and have only to regret, in doing so, that the legal members of the Board have given it as their opinion, that the examination of the same ought to take place at the College. And considering that these books contain a statement of the property entrusted to the care of the Trustees, and considering the irreparable injury their loss or mutilation would occasion, have also given it as their opinion, that the Trustees would not be justified in allowing the same to go out of their possession. In this opinion, with a single exception, the other Trustees acquiesced.

Still, as no formal resolution was passed inhibiting their delivery, I have not felt under obligation to refuse a compliance with your requisition. And though I am myself aware that the examination of transactions of sixty years standing, away from the place where the same were transacted, and apart from all those who have any knowledge of the said transactions, must be attended with great inconvenience, and may lead to unavoidable mistakes, still, in so far as I have had any connection with these transactions, I am glad that this is to be the case. I am quite willing to concede to those who have imputed a misapplication of funds, all the advantage in discovering such misapplication, which the most rigid scrutiny can afford, even in the absence of the party concerned. With so much of these transactions as have been made matter of complaint, I am familiar. If there be a wrong here, I am chiefly responsible for it, and shall hold myself in readiness to respond to any charge which may seem to be called for by even an *ex parte* examination.*

Very respectfully, yours,

ELIPHT. NOTT.

Rev J. N. Campbell. D. D.

* During the infancy of Union College it does not appear that any regular books were opened. Be this as it may, none were found when the writer of this became connected with the College. The accounts, however, appear to have been duly audited, and certificates of those audits have been preserved.

This omission would render it extremely difficult to trace all the transactions which took place between the College and the many individuals with whom it did business at that early day. No such difficulty, however, will be found to exist with respect to funds derived from the State. These have, for the most part, been received at a later period, and full accounts have been kept thereof in a fund book provided for that purpose, which fund book has, among other books, been delivered to Mr. Van Derheyden. In this book, separate accounts will be found to have been opened with each several act in which any grant has ever been made to Union College. These accounts will exhibit at a single view a full and accurate expose of all moneys received under each act, with the application made thereof. In the same fund book will be found a detailed exhibit of the present state of all the permanent funds. So that it is believed that it will occasion the Commissioners little trouble to ascertain the amount and application of all the grants ever made by the State, and the present condition of the permanent funds. E. N.

Letter from Philip S. Van Rensselaer.

New Hamburgh, Dutchess Co., *July 28th*, 1851.

Hon. Messrs. Walworth, Blatchford, Hunt, Wood, *Committee, &c., Trustees Union College.*

Gentlemen—I received on Saturday last the communication you addressed me as one of the commissioners appointed by the Senate to "perform certain duties in relation to the pecuniary affairs of Union College," requesting that the investigation should take place at the earliest practicable day, and apprising me that you had been appointed by the Trustees of Union College to attend before the commission and to assist in the investigation.

Very fully coinciding with you in the views you have expressed as to the propriety of a speedy as well as full investigation of the "charges made," and which I need not assure you I trust may result as you anticipate, I hasten to inform you that I shall by to-day's mail transmit a communication to the Rev. Dr. Campbell, apprising him of my willingness and desire to enter at once upon the duties assigned to the commission, and at such place as may be most agreeable to the other members of it, without regard to myself.

Very respectfully, P. S. VAN RENSSELAER.

Letter from David Buel, Jr.

Troy, *July 25th*, 1851.

Gentlemen—I have received your communication dated 23rd instant. I have had no communication with any of the gentlemen appointed by the Senate to investigate the pecuniary affairs of Union College, and am unable to name a time when the commissioners will act in the business.

I am under the necessity of taking an excursion with a part of my family for the benefit of our health, and expect to be absent until about the middle of August. On my return I shall probably be ready to attend a meeting of the commissioners. I expect to leave home on Tuesday of next week.

I am with much respect yours, &c.,

DAVID BUEL, Junr.

To Messrs. R. H. Walworth, R. M. Blatchford, A. Hunt & B. R. Wood, *Committee, &c.*

Letter from the Attorney-General's Clerk.

Attorney-General's Office, *July 24th*, 1851.

Hon. R. H. Walworth:

Dear Sir—The letter of the committee appointed by the Trustees of Union College to attend before the committee appointed by the Senate to investigate the affairs of said College, of which you are one, is received. I thought it proper for me to advise your committee, through you, that the Attorney-General is absent from the city, and is not expected to return until about the 4th of August. I will call his attention to your communication as soon as he returns.

Very respectfully your ob't serv't, W. BAMBER.

REPLY

Of the Trustees of Union College, to the charges brought before the Senate on the 12th of April, 1851, by the Hon. JAMES W. BEEKMAN, and before the public in the Albany Morning Express, May 8th, 1851.

To the Hon. the Attorney-General, the Hon. the Comptroller, the Rev. Dr. CAMPBELL, the Hon. DAVID BUEL, and PHILIP S. VAN RENSSELAER, Esq., Commissioners appointed by the Senate on the 28th of June last, to examine into the fiscal condition of Union College, this memorial of the trustees of Union College

RESPECTFULLY SHEWETH :

That having had their attention called to an article in the Albany Morning Express, in the words following—" *A report of the committee*" (of the Senate) "*who examined into the financial condition of Union College has been left with us for distribution: persons desirous of investigating a beautiful speculative scheme, can be accommodated with the material by calling at our office;*" and not having been previously aware of any *examination into the financial condition of Union College by any committee of the Senate* having taken place, or even heard of the appointment of any such committtee for that purpose, they requested of the editor of the Express to be informed *when and where and by whom this examination was made, and by whom this report was left for distribution.* And having done so, they learned that the report in question, in place of being "*the report of a committee who had examined into the financial condition of Union College,*" as stated, was merely a gratuitous *ex parte* report, made on the financial condition of Union College by the Hon. Senator Beekman, on his own responsibility, as chairman of the literature committee, and unknown to the College.

To the charges contained in this report, and in the article predicated on it, published in the Express of May 8th, 1851, an answer was prepared by the resident trustees, which answer having been submitted to the other trustees, at a meeting held at the office of the Secretary of State, June 27th, was by them approved and directed to be published. The publication, however, was suspended at the instance of the president, who presumed that the Hon. Senator Beekman would, on the presentation of the memorial of the trustees to the Senate, make the *amende honorable* for so unfounded and uncalled-for an attack on Union College. The Hon. Senator, however, on the presentation of said memorial, reasserted the charges previously made; and then as reported in his published speech, added, That

Charge I.

"*He felt it his duty to say, that he knew the half was not yet told,*" and that "*the truth had been concealed and kept out of sight, with art and skill, by the managers of the College Fund.*"

Answer.

If the Hon. Senator means by this, that the half had not been told The Public, in relation to the amount and intended application of the fund in question—a fund instituted by the liberality, and accumulated exclusively by the agency of the President of Union College, it is readily admitted. And what even now is said in relation thereto, is said contrary to the urgent remonstrance of the only donor to said fund, by whom the unnecessary publication of deeds of charity has not been deemed incumbent on a christian. But when the Hon. Senator adds, "*the truth has been kept out of sight, with art and skill, by the managers of this fund,*" if he means to assert that "the truth has been concealed by the managers" (*manager*, for the President has been the only manager) from the Trustees of the College, from the successive committees who have been appointed to examine, from the Hon. Senator himself, or from any one else who had a right to be informed, then he means what is at variance with his own published statement at the opening of his report to the Assembly, March 19th, 1850, entirely at variance with the published statement of R. H. Pruyn, Esq., on the same subject, not only, but also entirely at variance with the facts of the case.

For the proof of this see Appendix A. p. 29.

The Hon. Senator has in his possession, documents furnished him by the president containing a statement of every payment of every kind ever made by Yates & McIntyre to Union College, either through its treasurer or its president, and even of every payment of every kind ever made to the president on his individual account, with the date and amount of such payment, from May 31st 1823, when the schedules furnished by the Hon. Senator commence to the 15th of December, 1835, when they end. And the Hon. Senator is now notified, that he is invited to furnish to the Commissioners a single item ever paid by Yates & McIntyre to the President for the college, or to him on his individual account, not contained in the statement voluntarily furnished by him to Senator Beekman, and to every other member of that committee to which he belonged.

The charges made originally by the Hon. Senator, which on the authority of his report had been spread before the public in the Express, having been re-asserted, the board of trustees at their annual meeting in July, referred the answer to said charges which had been prepared by the resident trustees "to the finance committee, to amend and publish at their discretion."

The finance committee supposed that if an early opportunity should be afforded for answering said charges before the Commissioners, *viva voce*, any other answer might be unnecessary; but as this has not been the case, and as considerable time may yet elapse before such opportunity can be afforded, the presentation of some documentary information seems at length to be due to the Commissioners if not to the public. Said committee have therefore directed the treasurer to furnish each of the Commissioners with a copy of said reply; and that the merits of the case may be fully and fairly presented, to accompany the same with the report of the Hon. Senator Beekman, entire, (with notes and references. (See APPENDIX H. p. 83.)

CHARGE II.

In proof "*that Dr. Nott has been in the habit of employing the funds of Union College in his own private speculations*," (it is said,) "*here is an instance of misapplication. The sum of* $17,500, *received from Yates & McIntyre, was expended, as stated by the treasurer of the college on Dr. Nott's lands at Stuyvesant Cove.*"

The discovery of this imputed misapplication of funds, is stated by the Hon. James W. Beekman, to have been made during a personal examination into the fiscal condition of Union College, on the 24th day of May, 1849. (*See his report to the Assembly, March 19th*, 1850; *pp.* 44 *and* 48.) He now transfers from that report to the Assembly, (March 19th, 1850,) to this report to the Senate, (12th April, 1851,) this same charge, and reindorses it as having been found, among other charges, on re-examination to be "*fully sustained by the facts of the case.*" Thus reindorsed, this charge is transferred from the pages of this report to the columns of the Express in the terms above quoted, and published under the sanction of the same Hon. Senator's name a second time to the world. And that without an intimation that its entire incorrectness had been pointed out by the treasurer of Union College in his report to the Assembly, April 8th, 1850,—and so fully exposed that *that* honorable body declined taking any further notice of it.

Having thus repeated and re-indorsed this charge in the terms in which it was originally made, and in which it was transferred from his own report to the columns of the Express, the Hon. Senator introduces into this same senatorial report, two letters obtained from the private correspondence of A. McIntyre, Esq'r. Both of these letters, as will be seen, were written long before *the 24th of May*, 1849, on which day, the Hon. Senator, according to his own statement, made the discovery that this "$17,500 *received from Yates & McIntyre, was expended on Dr. Nott's lands at Stuyvesant's Cove.*" But neither of these letters seem to the Trustees, to justify the new phase, which is subsequently put on this transaction, in this same report, as follows: "*It appears to the committee on literature, a somewhat strange application of so large a portion of the permanent fund, to employ* $17,500 *for the payment of Professors' salaries.*" No wonder that it should appear strange to the committee on literature, that the same $17,500 expended on Dr. Nott's lands at Stuyvesant's Cove, should all have been employed for the payment of professors' salaries. Nor will this statement appear less strange when it shall be known that this $17,500 had not been applied to either of these purposes, but that the same was, at the time the senator made his examination, May 24th, 1849, lying as stated by the Treasurer, on interest in New-York, with Stillman, Allen & Co., waiting investment, as will appear from the following affidavit :—

"*City, County and State New-York:* } ss.

"I, Robert M. Stratton, of the city of New-York, do solemnly affirm and declare, that I am a member of the firm of Stillman, Allen & Co., of said city, owners and proprietors of the Novelty Iron Works, commonly called the "Novelty Works," and that I have the entire charge and management of the financial business of said firm.

"That on the fifth day of May, in the year 1849, I received from Charles Yates, his check on the Merchants' Exchange Bank of this city, certified by said bank, for the sum of eighteen thousand four hundred seventy-two dollars and eighty cents ($18,472.80,) which sum was received by me on deposit, and placed to the credit of Union College, of the town of Schenectady, subject to the order of the treasurer of said college.

"That there was drawn for and paid by me to the treasurer of said college, Alexander Holland, previous to the 24th day of May, 1849, the sum of two thousand seventeen dollars and fifty cents. That on the said 24th day of May, 1849, there remained in my hands to the credit of said college, the balance of said deposit, amounting to the sum of sixteen thousand four hundred and fifty-five dollars and thirty cents, all of which was subsequently repaid by me to said college, with interest thereon.

"R. M. STRATTON."

"Affirmed before me this 20th day of August, 1851, }

NEIL GRAY, *Commissioner of Deeds*"

CHARGE III.

It is said to appear "*from the books of Yates & McIntyre, that they paid in cash to Dr. Nott, for Union College, from the 31st day of March,* 1823, *to the* 15*th of December*, 1835, $802,323.28."

From this it would seem, that in order to ascertain the financial condition of Union College, this committee of the Senate, in place of examining the books of said institution, examined the books of Yates & McIntyre; and it must be admitted that they did so not altogether without reason, for it is a fact, and the Hon. Senator Beekman knew it to be a fact, that the former treasurer of Union College, (Henry Yates, Esq.) was sent to New-York (see Chanc. documents, § 92,) by the President, for the express purpose of guarding his rights and the rights of Union College, and that while receiving from the college his usual salary as treasurer and secretary, and from the president, $1,300, and his travelling expenses, annually, for performing these services, he entered secretly into partnership with said firm, and shared with them in their profits. He, therefore, (for he still continued to keep the books of Union College,) must know what sums were paid by Yates & McIntyre to the institution, as well as what compensation they paid him in the shape of profits, for acting in this double capacity;*still, if the books of Yates & McIntyre show during the years stated, that any such amount as $802,323.28 was paid either to Union College, or to its president for Union College, then they show not only what is not true, but what is shown not to be true, by the very schedules taken from their books, to the correctness of which they have made oath, as the same are set forth in a bill on file in the Court of Chancery.†

* See APPENDIX p. 64.

†For the PROOF of this See APPENDIX B. p. 39.

"*As an offset to this,*" (*the great amount stated in said report to have been paid to Union College,*) *the article adds*, "*the trustees exhibit property to the amount of* $604,350, *of which the college buildings and grounds make* $296,485. *The actual cost of these buildings was not, probably, over* $60,000."

Now, the old stone college edifice and its appurtenances, chiefly erected (but not paid for) before Dr. Nott became connected with the college, cost $66,618; that is, $6,618 more than the entire establishment is estimated to have cost.

Those gentlemen who have ever visited the grounds and groves and gardens belonging to Union College, require no other data to enable them to form an opinion of the candor of this estimate, and the justice of the censure pronounced in the Hon. Senator's report. To those who have not, the subjoined schedule (taken from the report of the treasurer of the college to the Legislature, which report was made the basis of the inquiry instituted by the Hon. Senator Beekman,) may not be unacceptable.

Buildings.

Three college edifices for the accommodation of students, including six officers' dwellings, the chemical laboratory, three society halls, college library room, and rooms for three society libraries.

Two edifices containing philosophical hall, chapel, theological hall, and three lecture rooms.

An edifice containing the geological hall and museum.

Two edifices, containing each accomodation for a family, a hall for boarding students, and additional study and lodging rooms, together with the sites, yards, and outhouses belonging to these respective buildings.

Grounds.

Four gardens in connection with the officers' houses, containing over five acres.

An ornamental and botanical garden of about eight acres, for the use of students in the study of botany, and of the professor of botany.

Extensive groves, and walks and ornamental grounds, for the use of students in exercise and recreation, and also for a college cemetery.

Also a site for an observatory, connected with about forty acres of grounds, and a dwelling house.

These buildings, gardens, grounds, cemetery, water works, &c., &c., amounting to about two hundred and eighty acres, lying in immediate connection with said buildings, and adjoining the compact part of the city, have cost (irrespective of interest) $296,485.31.

To calculate interest on one side of an account only, is believed to be not the most equitable method of making out a balance sheet; and yet, in exhibiting the fiscal condition of Union College, the Hon. Senator has charged interest on the amounts received by the college, but neglected, except in a single instance to credit interest on the amounts expended. How correct this method, of balancing accounts must be, will appear by merely calculating the interest on this $66,618, the cost of the stone college, from the time it was expended to the present time; for this alone would increase the credit side of the account some $500,000. What then would be its increase, were the interest calculated on the numerous other and much larger amounts expended.

Charge IV.

The Hon. Senator says, "*These payments*" (*that is, the payments to the other institutions*) "*were not made for the full amounts claimed by the college as credits; because in the case of the Historical Society the discount was one-third of the whole sum granted.*"

Answer.

This grant (which *it did not occur to the Hon. Senator to state*,) was a grant made without interest, and was not to be raised till after all the other grants had been raised and paid. So that Union College actually paid for this grant, including interest, considerable more than it was worth by computation at the time.

Charge V.

The Hon. Senator further says, that "*Union College received from Dr. Nott, without consideration, N. Bliss' bond for* $75,000, *afterwards exchanged for a deed of one-half of the Stuyvesant Cove property; that the other half came into the possession of the college on their paying the sum of* $58,632 *in* 1838. *On the* 21*st of July*, 1848 *the whole Stuyvesant Cove property was conveyed by Union College to Dr. Nott for* $177,587; and after the introduction of another subject, and a comment thereon, the report adds, "*the same Stuyvesant Cove* *property, one-half of which Dr. Nott conveyed to the college for* $75,000 *in* 1834, *cost him in* 1832 *only* $17,500. *So that he transferred to his own college, within two years after its purchase for* $17,500, *the same property at a price of* $150,000. (see page 97.)

ANSWER.

Was this statement of purchase and sale as entirely correct, as it is notoriously incorrect, the reproach, which to a cursory reader it seems to imply, would on examination be perceived to fall quite powerless on its object. For at whatever time and price this property was purchased by the college for $150,000, if within two years thereafter it was repurchased from the college for $177,589, the interest of the institution would seem, even in this transaction, to have been pretty well cared for.

But with what exactness the facts of the case have been stated, will appear from the following affidavit:

STATE OF NEW-YORK,
City and County of Albany, } ss.

I, Edward James, of the city of Albany, do solemnly affirm and declare, that some time previous to the 9th of April, 1833, being at that time book-keeper for Howard Nott & Co., I was employed in making up the accounts, and effecting a settlement between Doct. Eliphalet Nott and Neziah Bliss, Esq. That in said settlement, said Bliss agreed to execute to said Nott, in part payment for moneys received, a deed for one undivided half of Stuyvesant Cove, and a mortgage on the other undivided half thereof, which deed was executed on the 9th of April, 1833, and which mortgage was executed on the 1st July, 1834, as appears by the records of the city of New-York. That in this settlement, said cove was valued at one hundred and fifty thousand dollars by said Bliss, at which valuation it was agreed that said Nott should receive title to one undivided half thereof, and a mortgage on the other undivided half thereof, and that said Bliss should receive credit on account to the same amount, to wit, one hundred and fifty thousand dollars. And further this deponent saith not.

EDWARD JAMES

Affirmed before me this 30th
day of September, 1851, }

DANIEL W. MILLS, *Com'r. of Deeds.*

The simple truth in relation to this transaction is as follows:—

The president of Union College, to whom the Bliss bond of $75,000 (afterwards exchanged for an undivided half of Stuyvesant Cove) exclusively belonged, intending that the avails thereof, and of the whole Cove property, should eventually be applied to the furthering of the interests of "UNION COLLEGE, OR SOME KINDRED INSTITUTION CONNECTED THEREWITH," as stated to its trustees, in order to guard against the uncertainty of life, transferred this bond to the institution, and placed the same in the hands of the treasurer, subject however to his (the president's) control during his natural life. The other half of the Cove was transferred on the terms set forth. It being afterwards, however, stated to the trustees by Chancellor Walworth that the college could not hold real estate in trust without a special law for that purpose, and it being also found inconvenient for the college to furnish the means for improving this property, or to superintend the application thereof, the same was reconveyed to the president at cost and interest, being $177,887; since which the president has procured the passage of a law authorizing the college to hold such trust.

FOR PROOF of this SEE APPENDIX C; p. 47.

This transaction, so intelligible and so disinterested, was fully explained to the committee of the Assembly of 1849, of which the Hon. Senator Beekman was a member. As, however, the ultimate value of this property was as yet quite uncertain, the president was unwilling that any statement should be made to the public in relation to it; and, were his wishes consulted, not even thus much would now be said. His conduct towards the college has ever been such, and known by those connected with the college to be such, that he can well afford to "bide his time."

That Senator Beekman did not publish this explanation is no matter of complaint, for it was given in confidence; but, having been given in confidence, whether it was right in him to represent in his report, transactions so entirely disinterested and creditable, in such a way as to seem to imply a mercenary disposition, if not a criminal abuse of trust on the part of the President of Union College, is left for the decision of others.

It is left to the same decision, whether it was proper to transfer charges from his report to the Assembly in 1850, after the same had been refuted, to his report to the Senate in 1851, and having done so, and having thus obtained their reindorsement by the Literature Committee, to proceed, without giving the college an opportunity to be heard, or even a notice that any action was in contemplation, to report said charges as true, and to publish the same to the world, and this too under the imposing appearance of an authorized report of a committee who had been examining, by the direction of the Senate, into the fiscal condition of Union College, and whether it was befitting to introduce into this senatorial report of 1851 a document which the committee of the Assembly of 1850 never saw, and, having done so, to make therefrom the the following deduction: "*To the minds of the committee on literature, it seems not an erroneous deduction, from the preceding document, that, in the words of the majority report,* (*Assembly Doc.* 146,) *the president of Union College did use the funds of said college as his own interchangeably, as occasion offered,*"—especially to make and publish such a deduction, when, even though said committee had seen said document, such a deduction would have been then, as it is now, utterly destitute of truth. For though the Hon. Senator affirms that, "*by the legal document quoted,*" (the assignment of H. Nott & Co.,) "*it appeared that Dr. Nott was largely indebted to Union College on account of loans made by him out of the college funds to H. Nott & Co.,*" precisely the reverse of this was the fact; and had the Hon. Senator enquired, not of ignorant or prejudiced persons, but of the treasurer of Union College—he would have learned that in place of the president being in debt to the college, the college was in debt to the president; and in debt even beyond the amount of the stock transferred, and transferred for a temporary purpose merely.

Charge VI.

The Hon. Senator says in his report, "*It is extremely doubtful how far the trustees had the power to authorize their president, either to claim as his own so large a portion of the avails of the lotteries as* $111,343, *or to permit him to use the college funds indiscriminately as his own, so as to bring them in debt to their president in the large sum of* $366,177."

This, it must be admitted, is extremely doubtful. But it is not quite so doubtful whether the trustees had the power to authorize, or whether the president had the right to attempt, if he was willing to run the hazard of attempting, to save something for the college or some kindred institution connected therewith, out of the percentage granted by the State for the payment of managers and other expenses; and this is precisely what the president, at great peril, has not only attempted, but succeeded in doing.

For the PROOF of this, see APPENDIX D, p. 52.

CHARGE VII.

"*It is extremely doubtful*" *whether the trustees had the power to permit their president* "*to use the college funds indiscriminately as his own.*"

ANSWER.

However this may be, it is not quite so doubtful whether he had the power to use his own funds indiscriminately with the funds of the college if he was willing to do so, in order to save the institution from impending ruin.

What sort of indiscriminate use, by the president, of the funds of the college as his own it was that has called forth this rebuke of the Hon. Senator, will appear from the accompanying correspondence, from which the following are extracts:

"*New-York, January 4th,* 1826.

"Rev. E. NOTT, President of Union College:

"It has become necessary that we should inform you, that such have been our losses, *that we have no reasonable prospect of being able to pay the sum stipulated, or even to pay the prizes in the lottery now pending, unless we can procure immediate pecuniary assistance to a large amount.* If such assistance can be procured, we are confident that we shall be able to fulfil our contract with the college, and save ourselves harmless.

"In view of these circumstances, we have thought it our duty to propose, *that you and the treasurer should raise for our immediate relief, one hundred thousand dollars,* together with such further sum as may be necessary to sustain our credit, until we can be fully relieved, by converting our property into money, and collecting the amounts due to us, which are still good, but merely delayed in consequence of the general pressure.

* * * * * * * * * * * *

"With respect, we are
"Your obedient servants,
"YATES & McINTYRE."

To this the president of Union College responded in such a manner as to call forth the following reply :

"*New-York, Jan.* 23, 1826.

"Rev. and dear sir—I cannot omit, on the return of Mr. H. Yates, to express to you *my very grateful sense of our obligations to you for the prompt relief which you have afforded us in the hour of our difficulty and distress. We were, it cannot be denied, on the very verge of ruin,* and I am now, thank heaven, (if the Union Canal Lottery affords us the least sum we have calculated on realizing from it,) enabled to believe we are safe, if we pursue a uniform and prudent course, which I think we are fully prepared to do. We have had a lesson sufficiently appalling and distressing, to keep us in very constant remembrance of it during life.

* * * * * * *

"I am, Rev. dear sir,
"With very sincere respect,
"Your most obedient servant,
"ARCH. McINTYRE."

Within one month from this, as will appear from the following letter, Dr. Nott procured for the same firm, of Mr. Oakley, of Poughkeepsie, the further sum of $40,000.

"UNION COLLEGE, *Feb.* 15, 1826.

"Dear sir—Having understood that Mr. John B. Yates and Mr. Archibald McIntyre wish to be accommodated with the loan of forty thousand dollars, for one year, and that you were willing to make them the loan, but not willing to take the college as security, I have consented to transfer as collateral security, 179 shares in the Mohawk Bank; 20 shares in the New-York State Bank; 67 full shares in the Farmers' Bank; 176 do. on which $40 each has been paid; 2 shares in the Albany Bank; 17 shares in the Manhattan Company, and 150 shares in the Rensselaer and Saratoga Insurance Company; all standing unincumbered by any lien, in my own or my wife's right. I have also given a power to H. Yates, to transfer two bonds amounting to $7,000, which are abundantly secure, and payable at the Farmers' Bank. Mr. Yates, as treasurer, is authorized to execute the college bond, and I have authorized him to act for me in the premises, should any thing further be necessary.

"In great haste, and very respectfully,

"ELIPHALET NOTT."

T. J. Oakley, Esq.

This was the commencement of that "indiscriminate use of college funds with the funds of the President," carried thereafter to a much greater extent, and continued for a great length of time.

For the Proof of this see Appendix E., p. 57.

Still the Hon. Senator has somehow (unintentionally, no doubt,) precisely reversed the facts of the case in relation to this interchangeable use of public and private funds, and has blended both together in his reports, and thus given an air of mysteriousness and complexity to transactions otherwise as intelligible as distinct, and as disinterested as intelligible. And though the documents in his possession contain the proof that all the payments ever made by Yates & McIntyre to the president of Union College, even on his private account, have been reported to the trustees, and the report thereof accompanied by an expression of his intention to appropriate the same to the "*ultimate use of the college, or some kindred institution connected therewith;*" and that the President has long since procured the passage of the requisite laws, and made, under the advisement of Chancellor Walworth and Judge Paige, all the other requisite legal provisions for securing the ultimate application of these funds to the charity for which he has intended them, still, and as if the President were not at liberty to superintend his own affairs, or as if it were the duty of the trustees to interfere in the management of property to which they have no right, and over which they claim no control, and even as if his own duty as a member of a committee of the Senate extended to the interference with private property, the Hon. Senator has claimed to exercise the right of censorship over the acts of the President in relation to this property, as though the same were a matter of public concernment.

Why the Hon. Senator should have been so regardful of the interests of Union College in relation to payments made by Yates & McIntyre to its President personally, *in consideration of advances made, hazards run, and services rendered by him in their behalf*, to which payments the college never had any claim, either in law or equity, and at the same time should have been so regardless of the interests of the college in relation to payments made to its former treasurer, Henry Yates, Esq., to which the college had both in law and equity an exclusive claim, has not been explained.

If it was the duty of the Hon. Senator to inquire at all concerning payments belonging to Union College which had never been reported, *then was it his duty to inquire concerning said* PAYMENTS.

For the PROOF of this see APPENDIX F., p. 65.

Without wishing to detract aught from the distinction due the Hon. Senator as a legislator and reformer, pre-eminence as an accountant is not to be conceded. For however convenient it may sometimes be to calculate interest principally on the debtor side, it is not believed that such a mode of procedure is likely to recommend itself to the general favor, or to be adopted very extensively in the ordinary transactions of life.

The Hon. Senator informs the Senate, (Appendix, page 99,) that "*no portion of the grants of the State, was made to the President of Union College individually.*" And he might have added with equal pertinency that none was made to the Treasurer or the Trustees, or to Yates & McIntyre, or to any one else. This truism stands in immediate connection with the following untruth.

CHARGE VIII.

"*All payments from Yates & McIntyre, were called for as due to Union College, according to the statement of Mr. Hemingway, the book-keeper of Yates & McIntyre.*

ANSWER.

The entire falsehood of this statement will appear from the written stipulations of Yates & McIntyre—from their written pleadings in the Court of Chancery—from their written testimoney as a firm—from their written testimony as individuals—and from the written testimony of the Trustees of Union College themselves.

For the Proof of this see Appendix G. p. 75

The Hon. Senator begins his report in the Senate by saying: "*The committee on literature find that a very brief and imperfect inspection was made by the select committee of* 1849." and he concludes by saying: "*The report of the committee of* 1849 *seems to be fully sustained by the facts of the case, and the committee on literature feel free to adopt the concluding words of that report as their own, and to say that the financial condition of Union College is unsound and improper.*"

With how much authority this sentence of condemnation was originally clothed, as pronounced in the report of a committee to the Assembly in 1850, and how much additional authority it has derived from this formal review and solemn reiteration thereof in this report of a committee to the Senate in 1851, will be apparent by considering the following particulars.

1st. That both these reports were written by the same individual, the Hon. James W. Beekman.

2d. That no other inspection of the fiscal condition of Union College had been made since the "*very brief and imperfect inspection*" of 1849.

3d. that the result of that inspection, as stated in the report of R. H. Pruyn, Esq., chairman of the committee who made the same, was satisfactory; and, as stated in the report of the Hon. J. W. Beekman, a member of the same committee, was unsatisfactory. That to this report of the Hon. J. W. Beekman the trustees of Union College replied; and that, so satisfactory was that reply, the Assembly declined taking any further action in the premises.

4th. Whereupon the Hon. J. W. Beekman, having in the mean time become a member of the Senate, moved the reference of the subject to the Comptroller and Attorney-General. The Comptroller having reported that he had not been able to attend to that duty, the Hon. J. W. Beekman moved that the report of the Comptroller be referred to the literature committee, of which he was chairman; and then, on his own responsibility, proceeded to review his own former report to the Assembly, reiterating the charges made therein, adding still other charges, and ratifying and confirming its sentence of condemnation—and this without giving the college a hearing, or even notice that any proceedings against it were in contemplation, till said additional charges and the reiterated sentence of condemnation, apparently confirmed by the new sanctions of a senatorial committee, were published to the world.

That "the report" *of the Hon. J. W. Beekman of the Assembly*, 1850, should seem to the Hon. J. W. Beekman of the Senate, in 1851, "*to be fully sustained by the facts of the case*," and that the same Hon. J. W. Beekman "*should feel free to adopt the concluding words of*" (his own) "*report*" in 1850 "*as his own*," in 1851, and to pronounce *now*, as he admits he pronounced *then*, on "*a very hasty and imperfect inspection*," "THAT THE FISCAL CONDITION OF UNION COLLEGE IS UNSOUND AND IMPROPER," and that he should wish to persuade the other members of the committee to do the same, is quite natural. But how the other honorable members of that committee should on the ground of "*a very hasty and imperfect inspection*," made by a committee of another body, whose report had not been committed to them, have been induced gratuitously to endorse the same, and without giving the college an intimation of their intention to examine its fiscal condition—*should* "*feel free*" to reiterate the same unqualified sentence of condemnation, is only to be accounted for by the influence exerted over them by their chairman. And though it is understood that the other members of the committee did nothing more than to meet to hear the report read which had been prepared by their chairman, and on his responsibility for the truth of its contents, to affix their names thereto, still, it is not believed that they will on reflection feel, in doing even this, that they have treated Union College or its officers with that courtesy due to a literary institution, or with that even-handed justice due to all men—especially it is not believed that they will feel thus when they shall learn, as learn they will, that they have lent their names in support of statements which have no foundation in truth.

As if the gratuitous and injurious statements and insinuations with which this report abounds, might not otherwise prove sufficiently effective, their effectiveness is hightened by comparison. Hence the Smithsonian Institution is introduced. Concerning this institution, the Hon. Senator thus speaks:

"To show what a proper and judicious administration of such funds as have been long under the control of the President of Union College, (for his trustees seem never to have interfered with his financial designs) it will be instructive to look at the present condition of the Smithsonian Institution at Washington. James Smithson, of England, left his entire property to the United States of America, to found at Washington, an institution which should bear his name, and have for its object the increase and diffusion of knowledge. The trust was accepted by the United States government, and an act passed August 16, 1846, organizing the 'Smithsonian Institution.'

"The endowment consists of the original sum of $515,169.00, received September 1st, 1831, which is to remain forever as a permanent fund. The interest of this amount to 1846, when by act of Congress the funds were placed in the hands of the board of regents, was $242,129.00.

"A very elegant edifice has been almost completed and paid for, and the building committee have lately paid back a surplus to the permanent fund out of the proceeds of the interest set apart for the building, for the larger endowment of the institution." (*Report, Appendix, page* 98.)

Much as the trustees are gratified to learn the *present* prosperous condition of the Smithsonian Institution, they are quite unable to perceive the relevancy of a comparison between it and Union College.

Had the funds of Union College been put out at interest, ke those of the Smithsonian Institution, during the fifteen years to which the comparison extends, in place of being employed as received, and often in anticipation thereof, in the instruction of hundreds of indigent, but talented young men, many of whom are now serving their country in places of trust and honor, and diffusing abroad the knowledge thus acquired,—had the funds of Union College during these fifteen years been thus accumulating, in place of being thus expended, it might also have been looked upon by the Hon. Senator with a benignant eye.

On the receipt of this bequest by our government, $500,000 (says a member of Congress) were invested in Arkansas bonds and some small sums in the bonds of Illinois, Michigan and Ohio; in 1846, when the subject was investigated by Congress, little, if any, interest had been paid by Arkansas, and some was due from other States. And he further says that during the debate on the bill before the House, J. Q. Adams offered an amendment "*instructing the government to use moral suasion with the State of Arkansas and such other States as were delinquent, to induce them to pay the interest on their bonds.*" And adds, "*no fund was ever worse managed.* The Arkansas bonds are quoted as now selling from 53 to 55 per cent discount."

Be this however as it may, it is obvious that the capital of the Smithsonian Institution, which as the Hon. Senator states, was originally $515,169, ought during the fifteen years it was placed out at interest, to have produced at simple interest $540,000, and at compound interest $900,000, in place of the stinted sum of $242,-129, so boastfully brought forward as the extraordinary product of that investment, "*under*" what the Hon. Senator denominates "*such a proper and judicious administration.*"

Still, and notwithstanding this eulogy on the managers of these funds, and humble as the estimation in which the Hon. Senator holds the fiscal ability of the President of Union College, to whom the control of its affairs are exclusively attributed; and notwithstanding the pecuniary embarrassments these repeated attacks have occasioned, especially during the sickness of the President, (now happily restored to health again;) and notwithstanding the ultimate triumph and prosperous condition in which the Smithsonian

Institution is at length placed, still and notwithstanding these things, the trustees do not apprehend, even under the less approved administration of their President, that Union College, though but one of the many institutions founded by the Empire State, would suffer at present, by a comparison of existing funds, or of ultimate prospective endowment with even that proud monument of national regard.

As to the candor and fairness of the Hon. Senator Beekman's statements, or the authority of his decisions, whether as originally expressed in 1850, in his report to the Assembly, or as ratified and confirmed by the Literature Committee in his senatorial report of 1851, no opinion will be hazarded; still it is obvious to remark how very different the conclusions were at which the members of the committee arrived, who personally and carefully examined the questions now at issue, from the conclusions to which the members of a committee have been conducted who never personally examined said questions at all. The conclusion to which the members of a committee have been conducted who never personally examined said questions at all, have been the subject of the foregoing remarks. The conclusions to which the members of a committee, to wit, His Ex. Silas Wright, jun., His Ex. William L. Marcy and the Hon. John P. Cushman, after long and careful personal examination arrived, are as follows:

"In view of the preceding facts, it has appeared to your committee.

"That the embarrassments of Yates & McIntyre, according to their own statements, arose from speculations entered into by them apart from the lottery business, and wholly unconnected with Union College.

"That the President has furnished extensive means, performed important services, and run great personal hazards for the contractors on their repeated applications, and this evidently without any sinister motive, without the design of personal gain; but for the sole purpose of aiding the contractors, and of securing and advancing the interests of Union College, or some kindred institution coned therewith.

"That the course of the President throughout all the novel and difficult emergencies which have occured in conducting this whole business, has been marked by fairness and liberality towards the contractors, and by firmness, sagacity and disinterested zeal for the interests of the college and of education.

"That the full powers with which he was invested by the trustees, have been exercised with wisdom and success; and from the information they have received of his views in relation to this whole subject, your committee are of opinion that the interests of the college and of science, require that these plenary powers should be continued.

"All of which is respectfully submitted.

"W. L. MARCY,
"SILAS WRIGHT, Jun.,
"JOHN P. CUSHMAN,
"*Committee.*"

It is humiliating to be called on again to reply to charges, which, whether originating in ignorance or malice, have not, and have been shown not to have, the slightest foundation in truth; and it is also humiliating to be required to vindicate an individual from the imputation of applying the college property to his private use, while in the act of applying and periling his own property to rescue the college from the utter ruin to which it was exposed, and in which, but for his timely and disinterested interference, it must inevitably have been involved.

To persons acquainted with the President of Union College, and especially to those more immediately connected with the institution, any contradiction of the wanton and injurious reports which have been recently put in circulation is quite unnecessary. Throughout this entire circle the utter falsehood of these reports is well known. How they originated, and from what motives they were circulated, is also well known. It is believed that the documentary evidence herewith submitted, will furnish abundant proof to persons neither connected with the college or personally acquainted with its President, that the reports in question are not only not true, but also that the truth is usually precisely the reverse of what is stated.

Why, then, it may be asked, have these reports been permitted to remain uncontradicted so long? The reason is at hand.

The ruin to which Union College was exposed durnig the threatened bankruptcy of Yates & McIntyre, which the President had undertaken single handed to avert, rendered the utmost secrecy on his part indispensable. Not an intimation was even given to the trustees of the danger till it had ceased to exist.

A soon, however, as it had ceased to exist, the President informed the Board of Trustees of the fact and informed them also how that danger had, by his interference, been averted; what compensation had been proffered by Yates & McIntyre *for the advances made, hazards run, and services rendered by him in their behalf, and how he proposed to appropriate that compensation.* And though he took immediate steps to secure to Union College the ultimate benefit of whatever he might receive, still however, as the receipt of anything was contingent, and as much time must elapse before the amount could be ascertained, he was unwilling that his intentions should be made known beyond the limits of the board.

In the meantime he continued (by and with the advice of a finance committee appointed at his request,) to receive, invest and manage the funds thus acquired, till prevented by sickness from personally attending to that duty.

During this sickness, an act of the trustees gave to an individual connected with the College great personal offence. This act was imputed to the president, though unjustly, for being sick at the time he was not even consulted concerning it. The aggrieved party threatened to retaliate by placing the college, through the influence of friends, under the ban of the Legislature. To furnish a reason for legislative interference, a report (once before disproved) was revived and circulated among the members of the Legislature, and elsewhere, to wit, that the president had acquired great wealth by using the funds of the college in his private speculations. The real estate managed by his agents in New-York on Long Island and in Connecticut, and the stock known to be standing in his name, gave, (in the opinion of those ignorant of the facts of the case,) the color of truth to this report. Public prejudice was thus excited, and the threat which originated in private pique was executed. Legislative visitation was brought about. In what spirit it was commenced, and in what spirit it has been continued, the public are aware.

Still, the president, adhering to his maxim, that silence is the most appropriate answer to slander, and believing also that acts of charity were by christians rather to be regarded as private duties than acts to be publicly proclaimed, refused to give ; or to allow his friends to give, any explanation in his behalf.

In this refusal he has persisted, and though finally overruled by the board of trustees, the explanations now given are given contrary to his wishes. Nor would they therefore be given, were it not believed that the good of the college required this, as well as the good of other individuals concerned.

Though the documentary evidence hereunto appended has for the most part long since been placed in the hands of Senator Beekman, the trustees cannot persuade themselves that he has examined it, and it is confidently expected, when he shall have done so, that he will be convinced that he has been misled by information which though perhaps believed at the time by those who gave it, was founded on a misapprehension of the facts of the case, and that he has himself, therefore, in his report, unintentionally, done injustice to the Institution, and to the officers connected therewith. Should they however be mistaken in this, and should any further attempt be made to establish the injurious and gratuitous charges which have been brought before the public, all the Trustees have to request, is, that they may have an opportunity of meeting their accusers face to face, of examining the witnesses if any can be produced, in support of the charges in question, especially of examining the author of what is styled in Senator Beekman's report, "memoranda made by A. Johnson," which memoranda contain answers to questions imputed to the treasurer of Union College, and appealed to as testimony, which he avers he never gave, and which were never read to him, and which were distinctly disavowed by him in in his report of

April 8th, 1850, but which, notwithstanding such disavowal, have been reproduced as testimony in the Hon. Senator's report to the Senate April 12, 1851, and also of examining the books of Yates & McIntyre and ascertaining whether the $802,322 charged to Union College in Senator Beekman's report, page 96, (and on which interest is calculated and charged for 20 years,) is so charged in the books of Yates & McIntyre—and whether all payments made *to the President of Union College for advances made and hazards run by him in their behalf*, are also actually charged to Union College in the books of Yates & McIntyre, as they have been in the report of the Hon. Senator Beekman, and finally whether the books of Yates & McIntyre contain two distinct and different accounts with Union College, one from which the Hon. Senator Beekman has copied his charge of payments made between March, 1823, and December 1835—another from which their own sworn schedules of payments during the same period have been taken—the two differing in the amounts charged to the college by several hundreds of thousands of dollars. (As appears to be the case, page 44.)

All of which is respectfully submitted in behalf of the trustees, by order of the finance committee.

A. HOLLAND, *Treasurer.*

UNION COLLEGE, *Sept. 20th*, 1851.

NOTE.—The subjoined documentary evidence has been collected, arranged and printed by the treasurer, under the supervision of the chairman of the finance committee.

APPENDIX.

(A.)

" *The truth has been concealed*," *&c*., as stated in page 6.

When—from whom concealed ? *Not from Yates & McIntyre.*

Even during that critical period when Yates & McIntyre were, by their own admission "on the verge of bankruptcy," (and to sustain whom the President had generously put every thing he possessed in peril ;) those gentlemen at least were made acquainted with his disinterested intention of devoting the remuneration proffered him, should the same he received, exclusively to the advancing not of his own interests, but the interests of Union College. Hence, in a letter addressed to the President by Henry Yates, though he admits that he was himself actuated by motives of personal interest, he repels the imputation that such was the case with the President.

His words are : " That I, when risking the welfare of myself and family to the extent of what I have, should be supposed to anticipate in future some advantages, is not to be wondered at ; *but that you should be supposed to do so, individually, astonishes me. I have never heard it intimated by any one*, and I believe it only rests in the minds of some evil disposed persons, as what they or he would do in a similar situation." (*Chancery Docs.* § 119.)

In accordance with the views expressed by Henry Yates, are those expressed by his partner, A. McINTYRE. His words are : " But if the College is enriched, I rejoice in it, with the utmost sin_ cerity of my heart ; because I wish the success of the College, *and because I wish to see you enjoy that credit you so richly merit, for your able and unremitting exertions for that institution. I long for the termination of our labors, when it can be publicly known what you have done, and that you can have due credit for producing treble the amount of the College endowments that its Trustees ever thought of realizing from lotteries; you yourself cannot more rejoice in these results than myself.* (*Chancery Docs.*, § 360.)

And both A. McIntyre and J. B. Yates affirm under their sign manual, that "*the whole sum taken by the President was avowedly taken for the benefit and to be paid over to the funds of the College.*"

It was not concealed from the Trustees of the College. For as soon as the brightening prospects of Yates & McIntyre gave any reasonable ground of assurance that their failure would be averted, the President made the same communication which he had made to Yates & McIntyre to the Register of the College, to different members of the board, and even to the Board of Trustees in session, as will be seen from the following extracts: (*Chancery Docs.*, § 264 to 269.)

"Though the first payment of per centage for personal services rendered, and hazards run, under the foregoing stipulation of Yates & McIntyre, dated May 30th, 1826, was not received by the President of Union College until the 2d of September, 1829; still it became apparent to him early in that year, that there was a probability that the *apprehended ruin* of the parties concerned would not only be prevented, but that some benefits would arise to the College from the services rendered and the hazards run, by him, in behalf of the contractors.

"*It was, therefore, intimated early in the year, to William James, Esq.*, by the President, that the *funds* of the College would, *probably*, through his instrumentality, be more or less *increased;* and that, as life was uncertain, it had now become necessary for the Board of Trustees to *take measures* for becoming acquainted not only with their present property, but also with the nature and *extent of their prospective and contingent rights*, so that in case of his death they might be in possession of a *knowledge of facts*, requisite for securing the benefits intended to inure to the institution.

"Agreeably to the suggestions thus made, a committee of finance was, at his instance, appointed by the board, at their meeting in July, 1829, which committee say in their report to the board :

"'The concerns of the College have become large and multifarious under the auspicious influence and disinterested perseverance of the gentlemen who have heretofore conducted its fiscal interests.

"'Your committee freely acknowledge, that so far as respects themselves, they have not such a knowledge of the concerns and details as would be necessary in case of any adverse dispensation should deprive us of the Principal and Treasurer, to continue and mature their grand plan, without confusion ; they therefore request that such measures may be adopted as may appear to the board necessary.'"

To which may be added the certificate of Jonas Holland.

"I hereby certify, that on or about the first of August, 1822, I was appointed by the President of Union College, one of a Board of Managers under the act to limit the continuance of lotteries, passed April 5th, 1822, and Secretary of the board ; from which time I have assisted the President in keeping his accounts with Yates & McIntyre. That during the period referred to in the foregoing note, the intimation there said to have been made to William James, Esq., in relation to the contingent augmentation of the funds of Union College, through the agency of the President, was also made to me ; and that what was then intimated as doubtful, was afterwards, at different periods, distinctly stated as almost certain ; and previous to the stopping of the payment of the per centage as stipulated for by the contractors, *the President did, on several occasions, call my attention to certain documents relating to the said contingent claims of College from that source which, should his life not be spared to the close of the lottery, he said would be found among his papers.*

"JONAS HOLLAND."

"Schenectady, Aug. 1st, 1834."

(*Chancery Docs.* § 264, 265, 266, 267, 268, 269.)

"In July, 1831, the President of Union College reported to the Board of Trustees:

"That although contingencies might yet arise that would prove ruinous alike to the contractors, the college and himself, still they were apparently so far out of danger as to justify him perhaps, in communicating to them what he had previously more fully communicated to their committee of finance, to wit:

"That he had been obliged, in order to prevent the failure of Yates and McIntyre, and to enable them to go on with the lotteries, to render in their behalf, personal services, to assume personal responsibilities, and to raise moneys for their use at different times, and to very large amounts, *for which he was entitled by stipulation to receive a portion of the profits of the lotteries, should any arise, as there was now reason to hope would be the case, and perhaps to a large amount; which amount, be the same more or less, it was, and ever has been* (after providing for the services rendered and hazards run) *his intention to appropriate to the use of Union College, or some kindred institution connected therewith.*

"*That with a view to this, he had procured the passage of a law for founding, in connection with the College, an Institution of Science, the material provisions of which are as follows:*"

(*Clauses of an act passed April* 23*d*, 1831.)

"4. It shall and may be lawful for the senior trustee of the Schenectady Academy, residing and being at the time in Schenectady, by giving notice to the other trustees, to convene the same; and the trustees convened on such notice, shall be a board competent to fill all vacancies, at the time existing, whether occasioned by death, resignation, neglect, or removal of any former trustee; and that the charter of said Academy be revived and confirmed, any surrender or non-user to the contrary notwithstanding.

"It shall and may be lawful for said trustees to receive, hold and use, any additional moneys, or other property that may be subscribed, bequeathed, or otherwise bestowed for the purpose of establishing, in the city of Schenectady, in addition to the school hitherto taught, AN INSTITUTE OF SCIENCE AND INDUSTRY, in which manual labor, at the discretion of the board, shall be combined with mental application, by all the members thereof, whether preparing for college, for becoming teachers of schools, or for any other profession or calling in life.

"6. It shall and may be lawful for said trustees to divide such institute into such departments as shall be deemed expedient, and to prescribe the course of studies and system of discipline, as well as to appoint the requisite professors or teachers in each.

"It shall and may be lawful for said trustees, and the trustees of Union College, to make provision that the members of said institute shall be so far recognized as members of said college as to be allowed to attend the lectures and receive books from the libraries established therein, together with any other privileges granted to students in full standing, that may be deemed compatible with the interests of both institutions.

"The President further reported, that he had, with a view to the carrying the provisions of the aforesaid clauses into effect, purchased of the corporation of the city of Schenectady, the former stone college edifice for said institute of science, should the same be established.

(Chancery doc. §§ 436, 437, 438, 439, 440.)

In July, 1832, the President having in his report to the board glanced at the advances he had been required to make, and the hazards he had been obliged to run, in order to prevent the ruin of the college by the failure of Yates and McIntyre, added that, "while the affairs of the contractors were in the most unpromising state, an act passed the Legislature, authorizing the mixing of the land prizes in the Albany Land Lottery with the money prizes in the Literature and Fever Hospital Lotteries, provided the consent of the institutions interested therein could be obtained.

"This act of the Legislature, in the opinion of Yates and McIntyre, afforded an opportunity for making a contract which, though attended with the hazard of great loss, held out, as the alternative the prospect of corresponding gain.

"To enable them, however, to execute the contemplated contract, the consent and co-operation of the subscriber was necessary as the heavy responsibilities already assumed by him, in behalf of the contractors, must not only be continued, in case such contract was to be executed, but still greater responsibilities must also be assumed, in order to sustain their credit during the execution of the same.

"*To induce the consent and co-operation of the subscriber, a specific share of the profits, whatever the same might be, was proffered to him by the contractors.*

"Though fully aware that they were deeply involved, and that very large additional amounts must be furnished for their use, in order to sustain their credit during the prosecution of the contemplated undertaking, *the subscriber in the hope of ultimately benefiting the College thereby, made up his mind to put every thing at hazard, by consenting to share with them the responsibilities and the losses or profits of the enterprise, in conformity to the stipulations then made and provided.*

"This he did however with the intention, expressed at the time, and often since repeated, of *appropriating*, after providing for the expense and hazard by him incurred, his share of the profits, should any accrue, *to the use of Union College, or some kindred institution connected therewith;* an intention never relinquished, and which he still purposes to execute, reserving to himself the right of determining the objects to which said profits shall be applied, and the time and manner of their application. In conformity to which intention certain expenses have already been incurred by the subscriber, as others may hereafter be, in the enlargement and improvement of the College site, or the buildings thereon erected, or in furtherance of those arts and sciences which it is the object of the institution to promote."

(Chancery Doc. §§ 513, 514, 516, 517, 518.)

In 1833, the President reported to the board as follows:

"As to the additional lottery avails, arising out of the act authorizing the mixing of the Albany land prizes with the money prizes of the other lotteries, passed 1826, little need be said, as the rights and claims of the respective parties interested therein remain the same, as stated at length in the last report; no further payments having been since made to the subscriber by the managers, under the special contract entered into with him, by virtue of the act aforesaid, for personal services rendered, hazards run, and moneys advanced.

"*Of the several amounts previously received by the subscriber under said personal contract, held by him in his individual right,* though appropriated to public purposes, in the manner heretofore stated; *the principal part has with the approbation of the Financial Committee been invested in real estate situate for the most part in the city of New-York and on Long Island or elsewhere, or in bonds and mortgages, or stocks of some sort* and the residue appropriated to repairs and experiments.

"The old college purchased and repaired by the President, remains still in his possession; but he has not thought proper to proceed to the founding an institute on the amended charter of the old academy, to be connected with the college, as was contemplated, because it yet remained uncertain whether the amount to be received by him from the source aforesaid will be equal to his former expectations

"The subscriber is aware that the best devised human plans may be frustrated, and that uncertainty attends all things future. He is aware that contingencies may occur, that will not only refute the calculations of profits he has made, but also involve him, the college, and the managers in one common ruin. Still appearances are more favorable than on any former occasion; and even though the residue of the per centage, stipulated to be paid the subscriber for personal services, hazards and advances, should not be fully received; still there is reason to hope that something handsome will eventually be realized by the college, from the investments aforesaid already made, *and besides, even though there should be some deficiency in the final payment of the percentage stipulated, still the subscriber may, if prospered in some other way, make up therefor, and this if, in his power, it would afford him pleasure to do; nor will any thing but necessity reconcile him to the ultimate disappointment of expectations, which, though not founded on any legal claim, he has contributed to raise.*

"All of which is respectfully submitted,

"ELIPHALET NOTT."

Chancery Docs. §§ 550, 551, 552, 553.)

THESE REPORTS WERE ACCOMPANIED WITH PRINTED SCHEDULES (see §§ 289, 309, 326, 339, 371, 376, 391, 392, &c.,) CONTAINING THE DATES AND AMOUNTS OF EVERY PAYMENT EVER MADE BY YATES & McINTYRE, FOR ADVANCES FURNISHED AND HAZARDS RUN BY THE PRESIDENT IN THEIR BEHALF.

In all this there does not appear to have been any great "*art and skill*" *displayed* "*in concealing the truth*" from the knowledge of the trustees at least.

On the contrary, the whole facts of the case have been presented to them with sufficient frankness, especially when it is considered that these were transactions of a *personal and private nature, concerning which the trustees had no right to seek information, nor was the President under the least obligation to give it; as neither the College nor the public had any legal or equitable right threin*, as will be seen from the contracts which will be found under another reference in this appendix. Nor was this truth *unnecessarily* concealed from others. For the President did not hesitate to communicate freely in relation to the same, whenever in his opinion the interests of the institution required it, as the following letter FROM HIS EXCELLENCY, GOV. WRIGHT, to Yates & McIntyre, will show :

"ALBANY, 26*th Dec*, 1832.

"*Gentlemen*—To no cause or exertions do you owe the forbearance of the public and the Legislature, so much as to the manner in which the President of Union College has embarked his character, fortune and fame, for the sustentation of the managers, both against reproach and against pecuniary embarrassment. I think I have seen periods when the Legislature, regardless of other considerations, would have swept these lotteries from existence, had they not known that the doing so would bring ruin to the private fortunes of Dr. Nott, and deep loss, if not ruin to other fair business men, whom he had induced to lend their money and their credit, to prevent disaster in the drawings which had taken place, and to continue the system until the destined objects should be accomplished. * * * * * * *

"I am, with great respect,
"Your obedient servant,
"SILAS WRIGHT, Jr."

"Messrs. Yates & McIntyre."

(*Chancery docs.* § 528.)

In a letter to the President, after having examined the subject, the Governor writes:

"Washington, 15*th Jan.*, 1833.

"*My Dear Sir*—I sent you, some short time before I left Albany, a copy of the letter written by me to the managers. * * I have received from them an answer to that letter, and that you may be in possession of the whole facts so far as I am concerned, I think proper to send you the answer received. I feel the more strongly bound to do this, because I wrote to you as a trustee of the college, as will be seen by the language of my letter, and because in that capacity I had with you cursorily examined the contract and the correspondence with them, and from the facts drawn from these papers, had fully advised you to institute proceedings in chancery against them, in case they should persist in the singular position they had assumed. * * * * * * *

"I then say, that my impressions, drawn solely from the several contracts and the correspondence relating to them were, that there was not a doubt as to the perfect legality of each and all of the contracts, while I have always viewed, and I still view, the lotteries as a great evil not to be endured, but for the sake of the charities charged upon them; and seeing from the correspondence that the managers must have wholly failed, and consequently the lotteries wholly stopped, but for your exertions, I did think, and do still think it to be your duty to enforce the contract, that you may, to the extent provided for by the stipulation, indemnify the community for the evil continued by your means, by the addition to the charitable object provided for by the contract which induced you to use those means. My object in writing to the managers was, in a purely friendly spirit, to awaken them to a correct moral sense of the transaction. Having failed in this, I now give you my opinion of your moral duty, and the only condition upon which you can, in my judgment, excuse yourself from its performance, is that competent counsel shall pronounce it impossible to enforce the contract. Excuse me for this intrusion upon your time, and believe me,

"Your very respectful,

"And o'bt. serv't.,

"SILAS WRIGHT, Jr."

"Doct. Eliphalet Nott."

(Chancery docs. § 560.)

So much for the imputed "*art and skill made use of*" "in concealing *the truth*," as charged page 6.

(B.)

"*Dr. Nott received for Union College* $802,322.28," *as stated page* 9.

Union College "*received from Yates & McIntyre*, $802,323.28." So says Senator Beekman in his report April 12th, 1851, (page 96, 97.)

But what say Yates & McIntyre themselves, under the solemnity of their oaths, concerning the payment made during these same years, both to the Treasurer and the President?

They say in their bill of complaint, sworn to on the 12th August, 1834, before E. Cowan, "And your orators charge, that the annexed Schedule B, contains a true and particular statement of such moneys so paid from time to time by your orators to the said Treasurer of Union College, with the times particularly of each payment so made; and which statement your orators believe to be correct and true, the same having been made from their books, which they believe and charge were accurately kept.

SCHEDULE B.

A statement of payments made by Yates & McIntyre, to the Treasurer of Union College, on the fund denominated the College Fund.

1823.	May 31,	Cash paid	H. Yates, Treasurer,...........................	$4,450 60
	July 30,	do	do	5,365 30
	Aug. 2,	do	do	4,000 00
	Oct. 18,	do	do	9,163 00
	Dec. 11,	do	do	11,662 00
1824.	Jan. 22,	do	do	8,330 00
	Mar. 29,	do	do	14,543 50
	July 4,	do	draft to J. W. Francis,...........................	5,311 00
	Sept. 1,	do	H. Yates, Treasurer,...........................	17,958 60
1825.	April 13,	do	do	103,492 72
1826.	May 8,	do	draft to D. Boyd,...........................	3,000 00
1827.	Jan. 31,	do	bond T. Gardiner, with int. from 13th April, 1826,.	7,000 00
	do	do	Isaac Riggs' note, 10th Jan. 1825,...............	1,500 00
	do	do	Archer's bond, with interest from the 7th Dec. 1826,	16,000 00
	June 5,	do	bond of R. Richardson and wife,.................	4,000 00
	Aug. 4,	do	bond of A. B. Shankland,.......................	4,000 00
	Sept. 17,	do	drafts of Levy Bebee,...........................	3,682 00
	21,	do	do do	1,200 00
	Oct. 9,	do	do do	700 00
	15,	do	do do	1,500 00
	19,	do	do do	2,000 00
			Carried forward,...................................	$228,858 72

Year	Month	Day	Particulars		Amount
			Brought forward,		$228,858 72
1827.	Oct.	24,	Cash paid drafts of Levy Bebee,		683 00
	Nov.	15,	do do do		1,000 00
		20,	do do do		2,582 00
		21,	do do do		2,383 00
		25,	do do do		3,800 00
	Dec.	31,	do Levy Bebee,		488 25
	do		do note to Terhune, with interest from 14th July, 1827,		2,000 00
1828.	Feb.	11,	do Levy Bebee,		329 53
1830.	Feb.	4,	do note to E. Nott,		5,525 00
	June	4,	do note to H. Yates, Treasurer,		2,825 28
	July	3,	do do		2,841 88
	do		do bond of C. Barrington, and in. due thereon to this day,		18,654 17
			do J. J. V. Schaick, do do		1,373 62
			do S. Newell, C. Dyer, do do		2,062 33
			do Lyman Paine, do do		8,579 33
			do J. C. Van Dyke,	$6,020 00	
			Less note due 14th July, 1827, and interest,	2,362 00	
					3,658 00
			Interest on Smith's mortgage,		75 26
	Aug.	4,	Cash paid note to H. Yates, Treasurer,		2,856,80
	Sept.	4,	do do		2,873 10
	Oct.	4,	do E. Nott,		5,758 33
		18,	do H. Yates, Treasurer,		2,896 26
	Nov.	18,	do do		2,912 65
	Dec.	16,	do do		2,927 78
1831.	Jan.	18,	do do		2,944 25
	Feb.	18,	do do		2,959 46
	Mar.	18,	do do		2,976 00
	April	18,	do do		2,991 31
	May	18,	do do		3,007 93
	June	18,	do do		3,023 24
	July	18,	do do		3,039 05
	Nov.	15,	do do		1,230 43
	Dec.	15,	do do		1,236 27
1832.	Jan.	15,	do do		1,242 11
	Feb.	15,	do do		1,247 95
	Mar.	15,	do do		1,253 78
	April	4,	do do		3,187 58
		15,	do do		1,259 61
	May	4,	do do		3,190 68
		15,	do do		1,265 44
	June	4,	do do		3,315 00
		15,	do do		1,271 27
	July	4,	do do		3,128 84
		15,	do do		1,277 10
	Aug.	4,	do do		3,332 50
		15,	do do		1,282 93
	Sept.	3,	do do		3,177 88
		15,	do do		1,288 75
	Oct.	15,	do do		1,294 59
	Nov.	15,	do do		1,300 43
	Dec.	15,	do do		1,306 27
			Carried forward,		$365,974 94

		Brought forward,	$365,974 94
1833.	Jan. 15,	Cash paid note to H. Yates, Treasurer,	1,312 11
	Feb. 15,	do do	1,317 95
	Mar. 15,	do do	1,323 78
	April 15,	do do	1,329 61
	May 15,	do do	1,335 44
	June 15,	do do	1,341 27
	July 15,	do do	1,347 10
	Aug. 15,	do do	1,352 93
	Sept. 15,	do do	1,358 75
	Oct. 15,	do do	1,364 59
	Nov. 15,	do do	1,370 43
	Dec. 15,	do do	1,376 27
1834.	Jan. 15,	do do	1,382 11
	Feb. 15,	do do	1,387 95
	Mar. 15,	do do	1,393 78
	April 15,	do do	1,399 61
	May 15,	do do	1,405 44
	June 15,	do do	1,411 17
	July 15,	do do	1,417 10
			$391,902 43

SCHEDULE B.—*Continued.*

A statement of interest paid by John B. Yates, on his bond and mortgage of $55,000, *to Union College.*

1831.	Nov. 5,	Cash paid this day,	$2,656 50
	Dec. 3,	do do	1,005 50
1832.	Jan. 4,	do do	1,010 50
	Feb. 4,	do do	1,018 08
	Mar. 4,	do do	1,020 50
	April 4,	do do	1,025 50
	May 4,	do do	1,030 50
	June 4,	do do	1,035 50
	July 4,	do do	1,040 50
	Aug. 4,	do do	1,045 50
	Sept. 3,	do do	1,050 50
	Oct. 4,	do do	1,055 50
	Nov. 3,	do do	1,060 50
	Dec. 3,	do do	1,065 50
1833.	Jan. 8,	do do	2,996 44
			$19,117 02

The above schedule of payments, has been made from entries of drafts made by J. B. Yates, on the house of Yates & McIntyre. The whole amount of payments may not have been included, and possibly some may have been made on another account of indebtedness. By reference to the Treasurer's books and the statements, these payments may be exactly ascertained.

SCHEDULE B.—*Continued.*

A statement of moneys paid by Yates & McIntyre, for interest on a bond of the State of New-York, for the College of Physicians and Surgeons, to the New-York Insurance Company, which bond Union College covenanted to pay, and indemnify the College of Physicians and Surgeons against.

1827.	May 25,	One-half year's interest paid this day,				$600	
	Nov. 30,	do	do	do		600	
1828.	Aug. 18,	do	do	do		600	
1829.	Jan. 5,	do	do	do		600	
	June 12,	do	do	do		600	
	Dec. 7,	do	do	do		600	
1830.	May 26,	do	do	do		600	
	Nov. 29,	do	do	do		600	
1831.	May 23,	do	do	do		600	
1832.	Jan. 17,	do	do	do		600	
	June 6,	do	do	do		600	
1832.	Oct. 27,	do	do	do		600	
1833.	June 17,	do	do	do		600	
1834.	Jan. 4,	do	do	do		600	
	July 15,	do	do	do		600	
							$9,000

Summary of Schedule B.

First part,	$391,902 43	
Second part,	19,117 02	
Last part,	9,000 00	
		$420,019 45

Thus far from the sworn bill of Yates & McIntyre.

According to the summing up of this schedule, there has been paid to the treasurer of Union College, during these years, only	$420,019 45
But the two last charges in said schedule are *for $19,117.02 interest on J. B. Yates' bond of $55,000 sworn in said bill to have been given as collateral merely;* and for $9,000 interest on the bonds of the College of Physicians and Surgeons, both of *which payments were claimed to have been paid in error, and were actually repaid*, and must therefore be deducted, the two amounting to	28,117 02
Which only leaves to be accounted for, as set forth in the first part of said schedule,	$391,902 43

Now there was, (*Chancery docs.* § 58,) when this contract was entered into with Yates & McIntyre, July 30th, 1822, by Union College, due from the State to said college in its own right,....................................... $226,476 19

And in the right of the other institutions which Union College purchased out,........................ 95,780 62

Making,........................ $322,256 81

To meet this amount, together with the interest thereon, at the expiration of twelve years, the college received from Yates & McIntyre, including several payments of interest, only $391,902.43 as above set forth.

From the mere inspection of the figures, and without employing a skilful accountant to examine the details and make out an interest account, it would be sufficiently apparent for the common reader, that in place of receiving much more, Union College received from Yates & McIntyre much less than the principal and interest on the original grant made to it by the State; and much less than the principal and interest on the grants to the other institutions which said college purchased out. But to satisfy the Hon. Senator, that he has been misguided by Mr. Hemingway, such an accountant has been employed; and to say nothing of the labor and care which the supervision of the Literature Lottery occasioned, and nothing of the hazard to which the absolving of the State from all responsibility exposed the institution; to say nothing of this—that accountant having compared Schedule B with Schedule D, (see Appendix K, which contains, as will be seen, the final settlement,) found that the total payment of principal, between the 30th March, 1823, and the 15th July, 1834, according to the sworn schedules of Yates & McIntyre, after deducting certain small amounts of interest included therein, in place of being, as stated by the Hon. Senator, $802,323.28, was only $370,124.50; and that the annual payments in the abstract furnished by him, were in like manner exaggerated, as will be seen by the statements hereunto subjoined.

ANNUAL PAYMENTS

Of principal, including some small amounts of interest, made by Yates & McIntyre, according to the abstract from their books, furnished by Senator Beekman.

From March 31, 1823, to March 31, 1824,	$74,430 40
" 1824, " 1825,	39,286 85
" 1825, " 1826,	122,414 27
" 1826, " 1827,	46,436 60
" 1827, " 1828,	105,347 78
" 1828, " 1829,	
" 1829, " 1830,	70,037 88
" 1830, " 1831,	143,210 31
" 1831, " 1832,	116,548 82
" 1832, " 1833,	43,186 25
" 1833, " 1834,	16,340 23
" 1834, to June 15th, 1834,	4,216 32
Notes given by Yates & McIntyre, and falling due up to December 15th, 1835,	20,865 57
	$802,323 28

ANNUAL PAYMENTS

Of principal only, according to the sworn schedules of Yates & McIntyre, furnished from their own books by themselves.

From March 31, 1823, to March 31, 1824,	$57,414 40
" 1824, " 1825,	23,269 60
" 1825, " 1826,	103,492 72
" 1826, " 1827,	27,500 00
" 1827, " 1828,	30,295 78
" 1828, " 1829,	
" 1829, " 1830,	5,000 00
" 1850, " 1831,	65,000 00
" 1831, " 1832,	15,000 00
" 1832, " 1833,	27,000 00
" 1833, " 1834,	12,000 00
" 1834, to June 15, 1834,	4,000 00
	370,124 50

MR. GILLESPIE'S CERTIFICATE.

I certify that I have examined and compared the schedules contained in the sworn Chancery Bill of Yates & McIntyre, and those in their final settlement with Union College,* and have collated the same with their subsequent divisions and sub-divisions of the payments due, as stated in a volume of Chancery documents, and find therefrom that the total amount of the payments therein claimed by said firm to have been made to Union College, (irrespective of the $2\frac{1}{4}$ per cent paid the President for supervision and management, according to their contract with him, and according to a law of the State,) between the 31st of March, 1823, and the 31st of March, 1834, (deducting the accumulated interest on the delayed payments, and the interest upon that interest, included in said payments) is three hundred and seventy thousand one hundred and twenty-four dollars and fifty cents ($370,124.50.) WM. M. GILLESPIE.

New-York Dec. 11, 1851.

* See appendix K, Page 112, a schedule of the final settlement, appended to the sworn bill of Yates & McIntyre, (being schedule D.)

But Yates & McIntyre further charge in said bill "that they have also made to the President of Union College other separate and distinct payments in discharge of their obligation to pay two and one-quarter per centum, which payments are particularly set forth in schedule C, with the time of such payment, and which schedule C they also charge to be true, and which was made from their books, and your orators charge the same to be correct and true."

SCHEDULE C.—From Sworn Bill.

A statement of payments made by Yates & McIntyre, for the Trustees of Union College, to the Fund, denominated the President's Fund.

1823.	May 31,	Cash paid	H. Yates, Treasurer,	$1,309 00
	July 30,	do	do	2,754 50
	Oct. 18,	do	do	2,695 00
	Dec. 11,	do	do	3,430 00
1824.	Mar. 29,	do	do	6,727 50
	Sep. 1,	do	do	6,844 00
1825.	Jan. 11,	do	draft to D. Boyd,	9,173 25
	Apr. 13,	do	H. Yates, Treasurer,	3,849 75
	Aug. 6,	do	draft to D. Boyd,	6,844 00
	Oct. 10,	do	do	5,148 00
1826.	Mar. 18,	do	do	3,079 80
	June 18,	do	do	6,936 60
	July 3,	do	do	7,000 00
1827.	Jan. 31,	Bond, J. D. Hammond, (int. from 1st May, 1826,)		5,000 00
1829.	Aug. 4,	Cash, paid note to E. Nott,		5,350 00
	Sep. 4,	do	do	5,379 16
	Dec. 4,	do	do	2,733 34
1830.	Jan. 4,	do	do	2,747 91
	Feb. 3,	do	do	2,762 50
	Mar. 4,	do	do	2,777 07
	Apr. 3,	do	do	2,791 66
	May 4,	do	do	2,806 24
1831.	Aug. 6,	do	do	3,099 90
	Sep. 16,	do	do	3,009 50
	Oct. 4,	do	do	3,149 36
	Nov. 4,	do	do	2,024 69
	Dec. 4,	do	do	3,170 92
1832.	Jan. 4,	do	do	3,078 00
	Mar. 4,	do	do	3,048 52
	May 4,	do	do	3,078 69
		☞ ☞ ☞		$122,798 84

Schedule C exhibits the amount of the per centage granted by law for the expenses of managing the lotteries, which was, according to contract, paid to the President of Union College, (*Chan. doc.* § 36.) to whom the supervision and management of the same was exclusively committed, (*Chan. doc.* § 27.)

The whole amount of principal so paid, as stated by the Hon. Senator (see his report, page 98,) was $111,343.44. Of this sum (after paying all expenses,) there remained $54,455.14, as a compensation for services rendered and hazards run during the continuance of the Literature Lottery.

If the President was disposed to relinquish his claim to this per centage, granted by law as a compensation for services and hazards, he had a right to do so; but that the State should require Union College to account for this per centage, paid to the President according to law for supervision and management, would be sufficiently absurd. Not however, to insist on this; and though to the amount of schedule B, which, as stated above, was.. $370,124 50

there should be added the entire amount saved by the President from the $2\frac{1}{4}$ per cent granted by the State for supervision, which amount was,........ 54,455 14

Still, the entire amount received by Union College between the 31st March, 1823, and the 15th December, 1835, in place of being $802,323.28, as charged by Senator Beekman, would be, (even after this gratuitous augmentation,) according to the oaths of A. McIntyre and J. B. Yates, only.............. $424,579 64

Of this whole sum received by Union College nearly one-third belonged to other institutions; so that, including even all the President saved from the percentage granted for management, Union College never received, by many thousand dollars, as much as it would have received had the $200,000 granted in 1814 been duly paid.

So much for the $802,323.28 charged to have been received by Union College, page 9th and 96th.

(C.)

"*So that he transferred to his own college within two years after its purchase for* $17,500, *the same property for* $150,000," *as charged page* 13.

That these transfers were all necessary, and that they were all made in furtherance of the President's desire to secure to Union College the ultimate possession of the property which he purposed to bestow upon that institution, will be seen from the documentary evidence that follows :—

That the President purposed to appropriate not only his interest in the $2\frac{1}{4}$ per centage, but also his entire interest in whatever else he might receive for advances made and hazards run during the drawing of subsequent lotteries in which Union College had no interest, is apparent from his report to the Trustees in 1832, in which he says :

"For whatever profits shall arise from tickets sold in the Consolidated Lottery, over and above the original amount of tickets in the Literature and Fever Hospital Lotteries, reckoned at their scheme price, the subscriber will be entitled, by contract, to share the same with Yates & McIntyre ; and whatever the amount so shared by him may be, *it is still, as it ever has been, his design to appropriate the same in manner aforesaid; a design thus formally expressed that the Trustees may be induced to take measures for obtaining any contingent residuary benefits that may accrue to them*, conformably to provisions that will be found in the will of the subscriber, should his own life not be spared till said lottery is closed, and a settlement effected between him and the contractors, agreeably to stipulations formally entered into by them, and which will be found on file among his papers.

"All which is respectfully submitted,

"ELIPHALET NOTT."

July, 1832. (§ 522.)

And that he stood ready to carry this provision into effect at the earliest practicable period, is apparent from the following communication made to the Board of Trustees from the finance committee :

"Whereas, Dr. Nott has signified to the committee his readiness to transfer to Union College, not only its entire portion of said lands and bonds and mortgages, to be held in its own right, *but also the portion belonging to himself*, on the terms heretofore set forth in his reports to this board for the years 1831 and 1832, as soon as the same shall be definitively ascertained. * * * * *

"And further, that the Treasurer be also authorized to receive from Dr. Nott in like manner, the remaining portion of said additional amounts which shall be found to belong to him, and enter the same in a separate fund, to be denominated Dr. Nott's Fund, and to be held and applied conformably to the aforesaid report of Dr. Nott to this board, of July, 1831, and that a separate annual report be made, hereafter, thereon to this board."

I certify the above to be a true extract from the minutes of the Board of Trustees of Union College, of a meeting held at Schenectady, July 26th, 1837.

Nov. 28, 1851. L. H. WILLARD, *Acting Register*.

Why then was the remaining property alluded to, not forthwith conveyed to Union College? and why was the real estate which had been conveyed to the college in trust, reconveyed? The following documentary evidence will give the answer:

Chancellor Walworth's Certificate.

"I was consulted some years since by Dr. Nott, the President of Union College, as to the manner of conveying or devising certain property, to a very large amount, which he desired to give to the College, in trust, to establish certain professorships, or otherwise, to promote the cause of education in that institution, which property had risen from a certain per centage, which Yates & McIntyre had agreed to give him on the proceeds of certain lotteries, as compensation for his services and risks in raising monies to save them from bankruptcy. *I came to the conclusion that he could not convey or devise the property to the institution legally, upon the proposed trusts*, which were not such as the revised statutes authorized. And as he expressed the apprehension that he might possibly die before he could get a law passed authorizing the proposed trusts, I therefore advised him to convey the property absolutely, *taking such a writing from the treasurer or other proper officers of the corporation that he was entitled to control or direct the application of the property at any time during his life; and that he could, in that case, after he had obtained the passage of the proposed law, take a reconveyance of the property, and convey or devise it to the corporation upon the contemplated trust.* I also know Judge Paige was also consulted on the subject, and that he concurred with me in opinion.

REUBEN H. WALWORTH."

Saratoga Springs, Nov. 21, 1851.

On learning that it was doubted whether the college could hold property in trust without special law for that purpose, the President hastened to procure, and did procure, May 14th, 1840, the passage of such a law, in the words following:

"*The People of the State of New-York, represented in Senate and Assembly, do enact as follows:*

"SEC. 1. Real and personal property may be granted and conveyed to any incorporated college or other literary incorporated institution in this State, to be held in trust for either of the following pnrposes:

"1. To establish and maintain an observatory;

"2. To found and maintain professorships and scholarships;

"3. To provide and keep in repair a place for the burial of the dead; or,

"4. For any other specific purposes comprehended in the general objects authorized by their respective charters. The said trusts may be created, subject to such conditions and visitations as may be prescribed by the grantor or donor, and agreed to by said trustees; and all property which shall hereafter be granted to any incorporated college or other literary incorporated institution in trust for either of the aforesaid purposes, may be held by such college or institution upon such trusts, and subject to such conditions and visitations as may be prescribed and agreed to as aforesaid." (See note page 51.)

The following amendment to this act was procured to be passed by the President, April 21, 1846:

"*The People of the State of New-York, represented in Senate and Assembly, do enact as follows:*

"SEC. 1. The income arising from any real or personal property granted or conveyed, devised or bequeathed in trust to any incorporated college or other incorporated literary institution, for any of the purposes specified in the "Act authorizing certain trusts," passed May 14th, 1840, for the purpose of providing for the support of any teacher in a grammar school or institute, may be permitted to accumulate till the same shall amount to a sum sufficient, in the opinion of the Regents of the University, to carry into effect either of the purposes aforesaid, designated in said trust."

Having obtained the requisite legal provisions, the President acted in accordance with the same, as will appear from the following certificates:

Judge Paiges' Certificate.

"I do hereby certify, that after the President of Union College procured the passage of the act of May 14, 1840, authorizing literary incorporated institutions to receive grants of real and personal property to be held in trust to found and maintain professorships and scholarships, and for other purposes, he applied to me to prepare, under the advice of Chancellor Walworth, a conveyance from him to the Trustees of Union College of certain real and personal estate to be held by the latter upon the trusts authorized by said act. *And I do further certify, that I accordingly prepared such a deed of trust and submitted the same to Chancellor Walworth for revision and correction, and that the Chancellor revised and corrected the same; and that such deed of trust, after it was so revised and corrected, was delivered by me to Dr. E. Nott.*

"Nov. 19, 1851. A. C. PAIGE."

A. Holland's Certificate.

"I hereby certify, that President Nott, after having procured the passage of the act of May 14th, 1840, authorizing literary institutions to hold real and personal estate in trust, did employ Judge Paige to make out under the advisement of Chancellor Walworth, a trust deed to Union College of certain real and personal estate to a large amount, in accordance with the Annual Reports to the Trustees, made by him in the years 1831, 1832 and 1833; and that such deed was duly executed, acknowledged and placed in possession of the Treasurer of said College, with written instructions to deliver the same to the Board of Trustees on the event of his death; and that such trust deed has been, and continued and still remains deposited in the office and in the keeping of the treasurer of said College.

ALEX. HOLLAND,
Treasurer of Union College."

November 11, 1851.

It is hoped that the transfers and retransfers complained of (page 12 and 13) will have been, (even in the opinion of the Hon. Senator) by the preceding explanations, satisfactorially accounted for.

(NOTE FROM PAGE 49.)

An act in addition to the "act authorizing certain trusts," passed May 14, 1840.

Passed May 26, 1841.

The People of the State of New-York, represented in Senate and Assembly do enact as follows:

§ 1. Devises and bequests of real and personal property in trust for any of the purposes for which such trusts are authorized under the "act authorizing certain trusts," passed May 14, 1840, and to such trustees as are therein authorized, shall be valid in like manner as if such property had been granted and conveyed according to the provisions of the aforesaid act.

(D.)

"It is extremely doubtful how far the Trustees had the power to authorize their President to claim as his own so large a portion of the avails of the lottery as $111,343," *as stated page* 99.

FACTS FURNISHING THE SOLUTION.

On the 13th of April, 1814, an "Act instituting a lottery for the promotion of literature," was passed. In this act there was granted to several public institutions $322,256.81, together with the interest thereon for six years, within which time it was estimated that the same could be raised and paid.

Such, however, were the delays and losses attending the drawing of this lottery, that at the expiration of eight years, not even the interest had been paid, and there was no prospect of the payment of the principal within any definite period. In this state of things, and foreseeing that by losses and mismanagement the lotteries might be perpetuated through another generation, if managed by the State, the Legislature passed, April 5, 1822, the "*Act to limit the continuance of lotteries*," proffering to the institutions the supervision and management of the same.

This act expressly recited, that "*all that could thus be saved would go to diminish the loss of said institution.*" But as a clause was inserted, absolving the State from all responsibility for the ultimate payment of grants to the institutions, they were unwilling to run the hazard of accepting the same.

The Literature Lottery from which these several grants were to be paid, was, according to the Deputy Comptroller's certificate, (See Chan. Doc. § 54,) assumed to contain (§ 43 A.) tickets amounting, at their scheme price, to $4,492,800. And the allowance to managers for services and expenses, was $2\frac{1}{4}$ per cent on the successive schemes. There was due at this time (§§ 50, 58) to the literary institutions $322,256.81, to wit:

Union College,................................		$226,476 19
Hamilton College,......................	$45,279 74	
Asbury African Church,................	4,529 30	
College of Physicians and Surgeons, N. Y.,	33,971 58	
Historical Society,.....................	12,000 00	
		$95,780 62
		$322,256 81

As no interest had been paid on these grants for two years, and as the provision for the payment of interest had expired, the institutions being generally in debt, were greatly embarrassed.

In this emergency, the President of Union College proposed to purchase out all the other institutions, and having done so, to run all the hazards incident to the drawing of said lottery, with no other security for indemnity against loss, or compensation for expenses and services than the 2¼ per cent. already granted by law for that purpose; provided the supervision and management of said lottery was committed exclusively to him. Whereupon the Board of Trustees passed a resolution committing exclusively to him the supervision and management of the same, and vesting him with all the powers in relation thereto possessed by the board itself.—(*Chancery Docs.* § 27.)

And in the execution of this trust the President proceeded, on the 29th of July, 1822, to approve a contract (§§ 29 to 43) by which *all the right and title of Union College, in their own right, and in representing the other institutions, in and to the whole amount of tickets authorized to be sold by virtue of said act of* 5*th of April,* 1822, *was transferred to Archibald McIntyre and J. B. Yates.* In consideration of which transfer Yates & McIntyre agreed to pay to Union College $276,000, in ten years, together with the interest thereon; and to deposit in bank to the credit of the President, after the drawing of each class, *for supervision and management, the same* 2¼ *per centage which had heretofore been paid to lottery managers appointed by the State.*—(*Chancery Docs.* §§ 29 *to* 43.)

It is proper here to observe, that $276,090.14, paid down or paid with interest, is equal to $393,120, (the sum due the institutions) paid without interest in ten years in equal annual instalments, which was the time specified in the contract for the drawing of the lottery and the payment of the $276,090.14 stipulated. (§§43, 50.)

Such were the circumstances under which the supervision of the lottery was committed by the trustees to the President, and such were the conditions of the contract which he approved, for the drawing of the same.

But in the execution of this contract, owing to a speculation (unconnected with the lotteries) entered into by the contractors without his knowledge, they became involved to such a fearful extent, that the President was not only obliged to pledge his own private property, and the property of his wife, but also to implicate his friends in very large amounts, to save Yates & McIntyre from bankruptcy. As a requital for these personal advances and hazards, they stipulated to pay him "*such an additional sum as, together with the* $276,000 *which they were holden to pay, should amount to* 11 *per cent on the whole amount of tickets sold or to be sold in said lottery.*" (*Chancery Doc.*, §80, 81.)

Still, and notwithstanding the peril which this embarrassment of Yates & McIntyre occasioned, the advances it required, and the delay it caused, the entire amount of the grants, (which it was computed by the Comptroller would require, under the supervision of the State, *eleven* years to raise and pay, (§50,) and which Yates & McIntyre computed would require *ten* years to raise and pay,) was all, under the supervision of the President, raised, and the institutions settled with, the 2¼ per cent deposited to the credit of the President, and the lottery itself finally closed *in less than five years* from the commencement of said supervision. So that however doubtful, in the estimation of the Hon. Senator, the *right of the trustees* may have been to place the 2¼ per cent at the disposal of the President, (which but for this must have remained at the disposal of the State managers, who, after eight years, had failed to pay even the interest,) it does not appear that either the institutions or the public suffered very materially by the change.

But though, in the judgment of the Hon. Senator, "*it is extremely doubtful whether the Trustees had the power to authorize the President to claim as his own so large a portion of the avails of the lotteries*" as the 2¼ per cent allowance for supervision and management, (though the act of April 5th, 1822, expressly authorizes them to do so (§ 20), and though this is the precise compensation the State had previously allowed for the performance, without running any hazard, for the same services,) still, large as this compensation *was*, in the judgment of the Hon. Senator, (now that the responsibility had been transferred from the State to other hands,) it was not sufficiently large to induce any of the institutions, though greatly in want of means, or any of their officers, to run the hazard which, under existing circumstances, the supervision and management of the Literature Lottery involved.

No Trustee of Union College even coöperated with the President, or contributed anything towards furnishing the advances required to purchase out the interests of the other institutions, amounting (§ 58) to $95,780.62; nor, after they had been purchased out, did any other Trustee consent to furnish any portion of the large amount of funds required to be raised, or to share any portion of the responsibility required to be assumed to prevent the threatened bankruptcy of Yates & McIntyre, and the ultimate failure of the lotteries. This whole enterprise, which, by the other Trustees, was deemed too perilous to be undertaken, was undertaken and executed by the President alone. He alone, therefore, could rightfully have been authorized to claim this per centage.

But for what purpose did the President claim it, and to what object did he devote it? This question he has himself answered in his report to the Trustees, July, 1833. With respect to so much of this 2¼ per centage as remained after the payment of the managers, and of the other expenses incurred, he says:

"In relation to the President's fund, held in trust for the institutions interested therein, and which arose out of the Literature Lottery, afterwards merged in the Consolidated Lottery, it is only necessary to observe, that one portion thereof has already been paid into the treasury of this board; another portion deposited in the Mohawk Bank, and the residue invested in bonds and mortgages.

"As to the additional lottery avails, arising out of the act authorizing the mixing of Albany land prizes with the money prizes of the other lotteries, passed 1826, little need be said, as the rights and claims of the respective parties interested therein, remain the same, as stated at length in the last report." (*Chancery Docs.*, § 549, 550.)

It is hoped that the question so "*exceedingly doubtful*," as to the *right of the Trustees to allow the President to claim so large a portion of the avails of the lotteries as* $111,343.44, *as his own*, *while acting as the chairman of the committee of finance*, (as stated page 15,) will have been, (even in the opinion of the Hon. Senator,) by the preceding explanations, satisfactorily answered.

(E.)

" *The indiscriminate use of funds carried to a much greater extent, and continued for greater length of time*," *as stated page* 18.

" New-York, *Jan'y 23d*, 1826.

" *Dear Sir:*—Since my visit to Schenectady my mind has been in a very perturbed state, in consequence of my anxious apprehensions for ourselves and our friends. I am satisfied if we are sustained for six months, or at furtherest for a year, we can save ourselves, the college and our reputation. Our golden dreams for ourselves have vanished.

" With respect, I am,

" Yours, &c.,

J. B. YATES."

" Rev. E. Nott, D. D."

(*Chancery aocs.* § 90.)

" I acknowledge to have received from Dr. Eliphalet Nott, a check on the President's Fund for fifteen thousand dollars, and also his endorsement on three drafts on Yates & McIntyre for fifteen thousand dollars, one third at forty days, one third at sixty days, and one third at ninety days which is to indemnify him of the payment, and when paid, the check which is delivered to the cashier of the Mohawk Bank, is to be given up, the same being done to enable Yates & McIntyre to pay off their lottery prizes.

" *Schenectady, July* 17, 1828."

(§ 171.) HENRY YATES."

New-York, *Sept. 26th*, 1828.

Dear Sir:—We are now drawing to a close with our arrangements in consequence of our foolish and temerarious speculations; and we have entered into solemn written stipulations not to accept or become responsible for another without the consent of all the partners, nor engage in any purchase or speculation as a house. All, therefore, we have now to do, is to place our load in such a shape as not to be continually bearing upon us. I wish you, with my brother, would try to devise some plan by which this can be done. The banks here are getting tired of us. I think a bold negotiation for a loan with the means you have, would be a service to the College, as well as ourselves. You and my brother Henry are the only persons with whom I speak. The sooner a state of things is produced by which we mutually depend on each other, the better. We are now as it were on a magazine of powder, with a torch in the hand of a man who can blow us up at pleasure; and if anything happens to stop us, I am as well assured as I am of my existence, that no other lottery under the present grants will ever be drawn in the State of New-York.

"Yours, truly,

"J. B. YATES."

"Rev. E. Nott, D. D."

(*Chancery docs.* § 180.)

New-York. *Oct.* 8*th*, 1828.

"*Rev. and Dear Sir:*— * * * * * * *
I feel most sincerely *grateful* for the *liberal course* you have observed towards us. Without that liberal policy adopted *by you*, we should probably have been *ruined*. I cannot now, however, doubt of ultimate success; and I am well satisfied that *your liberality* has not only been advantageous *to us*, but in the end, it will be so *to the College*, and that you will have great satisfaction in reviewing what you have done. * * * * *

"Your very obedient servant,

"A. McINTYRE."

"Rev. E. Nott, D. D."

(*Chancery docs.* § 206.)

New-York, *Oct.* 25, 1828.

"*Dear Sir*—We duly received from Mr. Brown *the money left with him by Capt. Holland*, being the avails of the note discounted by you at the Farmers' Bank, Troy. * * * * *

(§ 215.) "HENRY YATES."

New-York, *Sept* 28, 1829.

My Dear Sir—We felt confident that we could get along without *troubling you*, but unexpectedly the banks have thrown our paper out, which discourages us extremely, as this is a very heavy week; we have becoming due the remainder of the notes assumed of Wood's estate, to the amount of about $12,000, and for Albany lands, and in all about $20,000. The brokers are not able to purchase drafts as usual, so that there is no *alternative but to* CALL ON YOU. I do it with *reluctance*, as we have had *five thousand* so recently, but since that have paid off a five thousand that was due in July, at the Commercial, and one of the same amount at the Mechanics' and Farmers'; we shall *want both*, and indeed I cannot see how to get along without. * * * * *

"I would not again *trouble you*, if I did not deem it *absolutely necessary*.

"Very truly, yours, &c.,

"HENRY YATES.

"Dr. NOTT." (§§ 276, 278.)

NEW-YORK, *Nov. 23d*, 1829.

"*Rev. Dear Sir*,— * * * * We received this morning from Mr. Brown $6,844.18, delivered him for us by you. * * * *

"A. McINTYRE.

"Rev. Dr. NOTT." (*Chancery Docs.* § 294.)

"NEW-YORK, *Dec. 23d*, 1829.

"*Rev. Dear Sir*,—Your letter of the 18th only reached me this morning. The proceeds of the Vail mortgage, *which you were so good as to provide for us*, have been accounted for or paid to us by Mr. Brown. * * * * * A. McINTYRE.

"Rev. E. NOTT, D.D." (*Chancery Docs.* § 304.)

"P. S. Mr. H. Yates returned this morning with the money you kindly provided." (§ 308 a.)

"NEW-YORK, *Jan.* 9, 1830, (*Evening.*)

"*Rev. Dear Sir*,— * * * * All the sums you kindly provided for us have been duly received, except that to be paid on the 12th, which we shall look for on Wednesday next.

"I did hope and believe that we should be able, by the 1st of February, to pay Oakley and Wilkinson the whole amount due them, or at any rate, so much *as will get your property released*. In this however I shall be disappointed. But those gentlemen have been informed by us, that we will discharge the debt in the spring.

Then it must be discharged; sooner it cannot be, which I exceedingly regret. * * * * * * A. McINTYRE."

"Rev. E. NOTT, D. D. (§§ 316, 317.)

"NEW-YORK, *March* 5, 1830.

"*Rev. and Dear Sir*,—Your letter of the 27th ult. came to hand yesterday morning, and WE RECEIVED, the day before, from Mr. Brown, THE PROCEEDS of the *two mortgages* which we sent you. The money came most opportunely, for without it, I know not how we should have got through the heavy payments of this week, amounting to upwards of $32,000.

"We are perfectly aware that you could invest your funds in this State AT SEVEN PER CENT, and if there was not a *positive necessity for it*, we would not ask you to take a transfer of bonds and mortgages received by us in the course of our business, bearing only six per cent. You know our situation, and that it is by constant struggling we are enabled to get along at all. It is *well for us*, and for you too, *that you take a right view of our concerns*, and afford us all the *reasonable aid in your power. Without that aid we should have been ruined.*

"There is one other mortgage which we expect daily from Philadelphia, of $3,600, and this also we must send you, relying on your taking it and *paying us for it*. I know we shall be in need of the proceeds.

"The 1st of May is the time which we allotted for discharging the debt of Oakley & Wilkinson, and to get *your securities released.* We purpose, without fail, to effect so desirable an object to you and to us, by that time. It may be that we may, before then, have bonds and mortgages which we may wish to transfer *to raise a portion of the amount* of this debt. If so, we must *rely on your assistance.* * * * * * A. McINTYRE."

"Rev. E. NOTT, D. D." (§§ 335, 336, 337, 338.)

"NEW-YORK, *Feb.* 2, 1830.

"*Rev. and Dear Sir*,—The $5,000 which you were so good as to send us, through Mr. John B. Yates, have been received. * * *

YATES & McINTYRE."

"Rev. E. NOTT D. D." (§ 322.)

NEW-YORK, *Aug*. 5, 1830.

"*My Dear Sir*—With the money I procured from you last week, and what we could collect from our offices abroad, we shall scarcely get through this week, having a very heavy week to meet next week; must therefore ask you to have *two more drafts discounted*, so as to have it here before the tenth inst., or one of $10,000 which Mr. Gregory prefers at 90 days; he thinks with ordinary success we can meet it. I am very sorry *to trouble you*, but I can see *no alternative*. I have dated the draft on Saturday.

"I am, very truly, your friend

"DR. NOTT." HENRY YATES."

(§ 383.)

"NEW-YORK, *Sept*. 11, 1830.

"*Rev. Dear Sir*—We are favored with your letter of the 9th, informing us that you had made arrangements for obtaining for us the $20,000 we wanted for the troublesome madman Vannini.

* * * * "YATES & McINTYRE."

"Rev. E. NOTT, D. D."

(§ 386.)

NEW-YORK, *Dec*. 30, 1830.

"*Rev. Dear Sir*—It becomes necessary for us, in the course of this winter and early part of spring, to pay Messrs. Seaman, Tobias & Co. $20,000 on account of a debt we owe them, and we are compelled to look to you for aid to enable us to do it.

"Permit us to request, then, THAT YOU MAKE US AN ADVANCE of the sum required for this purpose, on account of your share of the Albany lands. The payment *of the twenty thousand dollars may* be made to suit your convenience, either in instalments, or in one sum, the whole to be received by us, however, before the 1st of April. * * * *

"Very respectfully,

"Your most ob't serv'ts,

YATES & McINTYRE."

"Rev. E. NOTT, D. D."

(*Chancery Docs.*, §§ 416, 417.)

NEW-YORK, *Sept. 26th*, 1831.

Rev. Dear Sir— * * * * * The banks refuse to discount a dollar for us. We fear, therefore, that we may be compelled, however reluctantly, *to call on you for aid before very long*. * * * * * *

"We are, Rev. dear sir, with great respect,

"Your most obedient servants,

"YATES & McINTYRE."

"Rev. E. NOTT, D. D." (*Chancery Docs.*, § 453.)

"NEW-YORK, *Oct. 3d*, 1831.

"*Rev. Dear Sir*—We have for the last two months been peculiarly unfortunate, and we may, on this account, again be compelled to look to you for assistance to pay our prizes. We have several heavy ones now out, and among them one of $50,000. We shall avoid, if possible, to trouble you, but necessity may oblige us, and we think it best *that you should at once be apprised of this state of things*.

"The necessity of calling upon *you for aid*, is greatly increased by the money pressure now in this city. The banks *refuse to discount for us*, although we have not been refused before. * *

"We are, Rev. dear sir, with great respect,

"Your most obedient servants,

"YATES & McINTYRE."

"Rev. E. NOTT, D. D." (*Chancery Docs.*, §§ 455, 456.)

"NEW-YORK, *Oct.* 22, 1831.

"*Dear Sir*—We find that we will want *your aid* by the last of *next week*. There is more difficulty in getting discounts at the bank, and our prizes must be redeemed. Annexed I send you two drafts of $5,000 each; it may be necessary to increase it—if so, I shall send as soon as it is ascertained.

"Yours, &c., "H. YATES."

"Dr. NOTT." (*Chancery Docs.*, § 466.)

"NEW-YORK, *Oct.* 24, 1831.

"*My Dear Sir*—I find that the appearance of things to get aid here so much against us, that I am obliged *to ask you* to procure for us an ADDITIONAL $5,000, for which I send you a draft. I hope Mr. Boyd will be able to do it for the Mohawk Bank. This, with the two drafts for $5,000 each, sent on Saturday, I think will help us through.

"Very truly your friend,

H. YATES."

"Dr. NOTT." (*Chancery docs.* § 467.)

"In addition to $5,000 loaned to J. B. Yates on the 1st Sept. 1827, and $5,000 on the 14th of Jan. 1828, responsibilities were assumed in his behalf at the Farmers', Troy, and Mohawk Banks, as will appear forom the following certificates :

"Thomas Shelding,

"To Yates & McIntyre, J. Converse and others.

"1829, Aug. 13, due 1830, Aug. 15—18, ... $963 52
do do 1831, do 15—18, ... 1,026 52
do do 1832, do 15—18, ... 1,089 52

"Dr. E. Nott was endorser on the above notes.

"P. WELLS, *Teller*, *F. B.*

"*Farmers' Bank*, *August* 5*th*, 1834.

"Thomas Shelding—note endorsed,

"J. B. Yates, Yates & McIntyre, E. Nott, I. & J. Converse.

"Three notes endorsed the same.

"One payable 27th Aug. 1830, ... $945 29
"One do do 1831, ... 1,007 08
"One do do 1832, ... 1,068 80

"Said notes were the property of the Bank of Troy, and have been cancelled upon the books of said bank.

6*th* *Aug*. 1834. S. W. DAUCHY."

"J. B. Yates' note endorsed by E. Nott, for $12,000 was discounted on the 19th of Jan. 1831, for the benefit of J. B. Yates, in the Mohawk Bank, and paid on the ——

"V. FREEMAN, *Clerk*."

(§ 478, 479, 480, 481.)

"It gives me sincere pleasure, that we have been aole at length to get released your property, which you kindly hypothecated to raise funds for us in 1286, to save us at a critical moment from ruin the papers necessary to give you legal possession of your property, you will receive herewith. And now that this is accomplished be pleased to accept of my sincere thanks for the important service you rendered us in this particular, and be assured that I shall never cease to hold the favor in grateful remembrance. "I am, Rev. dear sir,

"With sentiments of profound

"Respect and esteem, your most ob't serv't,

"REV. E. NOTT, D. D." (§ 367.) A. McINTYRE."

"So much with respect to the "indiscriminate use of College funds." (Complained of page 16 and 18.)

(F.)

Then was it his duty to inquire as stated at page 19—*also page* 10.

LETTER OF JOHN A. DIX AND J. P. CUSHMAN TO H. YATES.

"ALBANY, *Dec.* 3*d*, 1834.

"SIR—In obedience to the directions contained in the foregoing resolution" [a resolution of the Trustees directing their finance committee to take measures to render available the claims of the College against any of its agents on account of receipts from the Literature Lottery,] "the FINANCE COMMITTEE have had the subject under examination; and they perceive that you were authorised by their resolution of the 24th July, 1822, in relation to the Literature Lottery, to perform certain acts in behalf of the Trustees of the College, as their treasurer under the supervision of the president; that you went in that capacity, with the consent of the president, to the city of New-York; that while there you received your salary from the College, and that other allowances were also made to you for your services and expenses. The committee have recently learned that while acting in that capacity, you became a partner of the firm of Yates & McIntyre, and interested in their profits. The committee conceive that among the rights acquired by the College, are those which have grown out of your proceedings, in becoming interested in the management and drawing of the lotteries while employed and acting as the agent of Uunion College; and your participation, while so employed in the profits of the lotteries, in which the College was interested; and we deem it our duty to apprize you, that we claim these profits as rightfully belonging to the College.

"We have therefore respectfully to ask, that you will furnish the committee with a copy of the articles of co-partnership entered into between you and the house of Yates & McIntyre, referred to in their bill of complaint recently filed against the trustees of the College, together with a statement of all your operations in pursuance of those articles of co-partnership; that you will also furnish them with a full and detailed account of all moneys, stock and other property received by you from the profits of said co-partnership, or in any way growing out of said connection; and that you will also furnish a detailed account of all moneys, stocks and other property, in which you have in any form become interested, by virtue of your said co-partnership connection with said house during your said agency.

"We are very respectfully, yours &c.,

(Signed) JOHN A. DIX,

JOHN P. CUSHMAN,

in behalf of the finance committee."

Immediately after the President had assumed the requested responsibilities, and assisted in raising the requisite funds for preventing the threatened bankruptcy of Yates & McIntyre, A. McIntyre, one of the partners, writes the President, January 23d, 1826, as follows :—

(*Chancery Docs.* § 86 and 87.)

"We have had a lesson sufficiently appalling and distressing to keep us in very constant remembrance of it during life."

"As, however, I am more than ever sensible of the frailty of human nature, and the uncertainty of all earthly calculations, I am anxious, above all things in this world, to get through with our present engagements without ruin to ourselves and our friends; and I have thought that *the presence and advice of Mr. Henry Yates here*, for as much of his time as he could possibly spare with us might be useful. He has consented to come, and we shall provide as liberally as we can for his sacrifice. Perhaps you too can, with propriety, make him an allowance, on account of the INCREASED SAFETY OF THE COLLEGE."

On the same day J. B. Yates, the only other partner, writes the President as follows :

(*Chancery Docs.* § 90.)

"I AM SATISFIED IF WE ARE SUSTAINED FOR SIX MONTHS, *or at the furthest, for one year, we can save our friends, the college, and our reputation. Our golden dreams for ourselves have vanished*, and with them all the imagined good I thought of doing with it. Still, a comfortable competence is far from hopeless. I do not know what further you may have in your power, should it become requisite. On mature reflection, I am convinced that our safety requires that I should go south if we continue operating; and in that event, I KNOW THE PRESENCE OF MY BROTHER, AS TREAS-

URER OF THE COLLEGE, *during the whole time, to see to things and aid with all the energy he possesses, is positively necessary, for a variety of reasons.* Mr. McIntyre and I must now necessarily both be often and long absent, and often unexpectedly, and we will need his active aid, besides the *beneficial public effect it would have, that he is known to be here as the treasurer of the college.*"

"After reflecting upon the contents of the above letters, and for the express purpose of more effectually guarding the rights, and furthering the interests of Union College, the President employed Mr. H. Yates, at the time treasurer and clerk of the board, and soon thereafter a trustee, to go to New-York as agent of the college, and to remain there as much of the time as practicable, until the close of the Literature Lottery, and agreed to continue to pay him during his absence (besides his salary as treasurer and clerk, which he retained) the sum of $1,300 per annum, and also to pay his traveling expenses, &c., while absent."

(*Chancery Docs.* § 91, 92.)

Why Yates & McIntyre were so desirous to have Henry Yates sent to New-York to look after the interests of Union College, AS ITS TREASURER, and how exclusively he devoted himself to the promotion of those interests, and to what extent he ultimately contributed to the promotion of the same, will appear from the following correspondence :—

On the 15th of May, 1830, A. McIntyre writes to the President as follows :

'I am sensible that our contracts have had to be varied and modified from time to time, and that the changes *have given you trouble and vexation*, but a change of times and circumstances rendered them necessary. They were unavoidable, *and had you pursued a less liberal and just policy, you would have disheartened and ruined us, and inflicted a serious injury on the college.* And I consider the change now asked for of a similar character with those formerly asked for and granted. *I hope and trust, however, that this may be the last that we shall ever be compelled to sue for.* I certainly shall never ask for another, unless dire necessity compels me. I dare not say the necessity may not come. I mean, however, to *say, emphatically, that necessity alone shall ever compel me to ask any other change or concession.*

"Allow me to hope, then, that you will make this one further change. I entreat that you do."

(*Chancery Docs.*, § 362.)

On the 15th of July, 1830, a new stipulation was entered into in the words following, containing the concession so urgently desired:

(*Chancery Docs.*, § 378.)

"Whereas, the *claims of Union College against the subscribers, Yates & McIntyre, arising out of their contracts under the law to limit the continuance of lotteries*, passed the 5th April, 1822, *have been fully paid* or provided for by notes given August 1st, 1828, *when said contract was cancelled;* and whereas, the stipulation of the subscribers, entered into with *Eliphalet Nott, on the* 30*th May*, 1826, under the "act to enable the mayor, aldermen, and commonalty of the city of Albany to dispose of tickets in a lottery heretofore granted, and to limit the continuance of the same," passed April 13th, 1826, *was for and in consideration of personal services rendered, or to be rendered, and hazards run on our account;* and whereas, the hazards are diminishing, while the difficulties of conducting the lotteries are increasing; therefore, *in lieu of said stipulation, entered into on the* 30*th May*, 1826, *and of all the personal demands arising as aforesaid, out of services rendered and hazards run by said Nott for us*, in regard to so much of the Consolidated Lottery as shall have been, or to be drawn from and after the first day of May last, the subscribers promise to pay to said Eliphalet Nott, within ninety days from the drawing of each class, drawn as aforesaid, after the first of May last, *five per centum on the gross amount of tickets sold therein*,* after deducting therefrom the contained amount of land, if any, in any of the schemes: it being always understood that the said Eliphalet Nott is to take an equal share with us of the Albany lands that may fall into our hands by purchase or by drawing them on hand at the price they may cost us, and allowing us interest on the

* In place of 6 31-100 per cent. which they were previously bound to pay.

cost from the time of payment; and also that we are to continue to be authorized to sell any such Albany lands, when we can do so, we to be accountable to them therefor.

"YATES & McINTYRE."

New-York, *July* 15, 1830.

(*Chanc. doc.* § 375.)

On the 27th of April, 1832, Mr. Henry Yates, still treasurer of Union College, and under pay for attending to its interests, writes to the President as follows:

(*Chancery doc.* § 482.)

"*My Dear Sir*—We have this morning had a short conversation on the subject of our finances and future operations. It will be necessary for you *to make up your mind not to draw any more money from here* (except the sum to be paid to-day.) Probably some of the partners will write to you more particularly, as to the course we mean to pursue.

"Very truly your friend,

H. YATES."

On the 28th of April, 1832, Henry Yates, Treasurer of Union College, in connection with two other persons, till then unknown as connected with the lottery, writes to the President as follows:

(*Chancery docs.* §§ 485 to 491.)

"*Rev. and Dear Sir*—We are obliged, by circumstances, to ad dress you on a subject that our partners have examined with you, but in which you and they have had erroneous impressions. We allude here to the profits on the lotteries. Your calculations in relation to these profits, however true in theory, have proved fallacious when tested by actual experiment. It doubtless was one of the great causes of our partners getting so much in arrears, in the first three years of their operations under the present system of lotteries.*

* The partners themselves attributed their embarrassments to a very different cause to wit: to their unwarrantable speculations.

"In Philadelphia the same mistake was made, but the mode was subsequently changed, and instead of a per centage, an annual stipend was paid, so as to recover from the losses sustained there, which, with the more advantageous contracts which we have taken in other States, has enabled us to bear up against difficulties here.

"In consequence of your individual exertions, your enlightened views of the whole affair, and continued efforts to aid the house, we, or some of us, at least, have heretofore consented to pay far more than ever could have been contemplated, amounting at least under different heads, to —— (No amount was mentioned.)

"Having done this, we must ask you not only to continue your friendly aid, but to relinquish any further claim on us. What is done we shall endeavor not to recall, if circumstances are such as to avoid it. The last allowance, though large, can only be considered as a gratuity, and never would be tolerated if known.

"The step which we now take is not intended for our own benefit, but to provide for the losses which were sustained before we entered into the concern. So much was lost, and such amounts paid to the institution for which you acted, that the then managers owed much more than they had assets to pay. This being charged to them, will reduce their share of any profits that have been subsequently made, and would possibly reduce what they have yet to a mere pittance, if anything.

"We consider the full value of a lottery no more than five per cent. on the sales.* That sum we propose to allow them in New-York. We deem that we have purchased both but having made the institutions an extra allowance, we have determined to allow John B. Yates and Archibald McIntyre,† the same for the

* The real value is 15 per cent, that being the per centage deducted according to law.

† The very individuals, and the only individuals who were parties to the contracts with the College and its President.

time yet to come, particularly as we are satisfied it will be wanted to make them whole.

Dated at New-York, April 18, 1832.

"We are, reverend sir,

"With the greatest respect,

"Your obedient servants,

"H. YATES,

"JOHN ELY, Jr.

"JAMES McINTYRE,

"by JOHN ELY, Jr.*"

"Rev. Dr. Eliphalet Nott."

...

"Whatever the circumstance may have been which led to the foregoing refusal, it would seem, from the abstract (*Chancery docs.* §248,) that neither a diminution of sales nor inadequacy of compensation, could be among them.

"Though the falling off of the lottery business, so much complained of in the foregoing correspondence, were not contradicted by the actual returns from time to time obtained, still it would be apparent, from the general tenor thereof, that said correspondence was conducted, on the part of the contractors, during the latter periods, with a view to *effect*, rather than to a full and fair exposure of their profits and losses. For though said correspondence abounds with references to frequent *unfortunate* drawings, it omits to mention the no less frequent *fortunate* drawings, which must, as admitted by Yates & McIntyre, (*Chancery docs.* § 236 *also* § 328,) have occurred; and of which so much was heard from another quarter.

"Indeed after the original hope of acquiring fortunes began to revive in the minds of the contractors, it was deemed needful, on account of public opinion, for them to expose, without reserve, their former losses, and conceal as far as practicable, their progressive gains.

..

"That they were embarrassed, and sometimes greatly, until near the time of their refusal to fulfill their engagements, is not

* Mr. James McIntyre is incapable of signing his name at present, having severely sprained his wrist by a fall from a horse. He therefore requested his friend, J. Ely, jr., to sign for him.

doubted. How should it be otherwise? Neither of them were in independent circumstances when the original contract was entered into. On the contrary both were known to be embarrassed. And yet after making that contract, besides stock to a very large amount in the Welland canal, the Union canal, the Morris canal, the Arcade, Philadelphia, and Utica Insurance Company, and sundry other incorporated companies, they purchased real estate in the city of Washington, in the State of Pennsylvania, to a large amount in the State of New-Jersey, and in the city of Albany to a large amount, and in the city of New-York to a still larger amount, where large sums were also expended in building.

"All these purchases required to be paid for out of the avails of the lotteries; and being paid for, (as they have been to a considerable extent, with a portion of the profits belonging to the college,) they have left the contractors, exclusive of other gains in the possession of a great estate.

(*Chanc. doc*, §§ 492 to 496.)

Dr. Nott to Yates & McIntyre.

"WAY, 10*th May*, 1832.

"*Gentlemen*—A communication expressive, as it seems to me, of a determination on the part of THIRD PERSONS to interfere with our reciprocal rights and duties, has been received. Nothing but an apprehension, either that I have misunderstood the import and design of this communication, or that the persons making it were at the time laboring under some strange delusion, either having forgotten, or not having previously known, that every material fact stated is disproved, and every opinion expressed refuted, by indisputable evidence in my own possession, could render any answer on my part consistent *with self respect*.

"It is my design to send to you a copy of this (to me) unaccountable communication, together with the reply thereto, should any reply, on reflection, be deemed requisite, as soon as I am able.

"At present I am travelling for my health: I shall, however, I hope, be home in a week or ten days, by which time, I trust, the regular returns will be made out and forwarded, that there may be no further delay in the payments stipulated to be made, as the same become due; for which I shall draw as usual, unless you prefer to deposit the amount to my credit in the Manhattan bank, and give me notice thereof, which you are hereby authorized to do.

"Very respectfully,

"E. NOTT."

"Messrs. YATES & McINTYRE."

(*Chancery Doc.*, § 497.)

Yates & McIntyre to Dr. Nott.

NEW-YORK, *May* 15*th*, 1832.

"*Rev. Sir*—Your letter of the tenth was received last evening. The communication to which you allude, is that of a portion of the house of Yates & McIntyre, not of third persons,* and although not the direct act of the whole house, yet the purport of it was communicated to all, and all acceded to its being made to you.

"*The simple truth of the matter is this: All the members of the house have uniformly been very willing to sanction and give full effect to your views of the arrangement between us (except Mr. J. B. Yates) however contrary such acquiescence might be to what they considered their legal rights.* They did so with the sincerest pleasure, and would probably have continued to do so until the conclusion of their lottery labors, were it not that on a more correct and narrow view of our concerns, connected with THE CERTAIN AND EARLY CLOSE† of our business, they can plainly see that they

* So it is now admitted, and by a bill in Chancery afterwards proved, that the treasurer of Union College, Henry Yates, Esq., on going to New-York, July 1st, 1826, as the paid agent of the College and its President, to protect their rights, immediately entered into partnership with Yates & McIntyre; and that he has ever since continued to act in the double capacity of treasurer of the College and partner in said firm; and now, with two other persons, like himself unknown to Union College as partners, comes forward, a self-constituted umpire, and decides that the per centage promised to be paid by Archibald McIntyre, and his brother J. B. Yates, to Eliphalet Nott, for moneys advanced, hazards run, and services rendered by him in their behalf, shall now be taken from the said Eliphalet Nott and given to the said Archibald McIntyre and J. B. Yates, who originally promised to pay the same to said Nott.

† Mr. J. B. Yates having just concluded an agreement to close the lottery with the year 1833.

will end with a *scanty remuneration;* and this they think would particularly be the case with the *two first who engaged in the business.*

"Those two (J. B. Yates and A. McIntyre) suffered appalling and ruinous losses, *in acquiring that knowledge and experience** in the business which was so necessary to its successful prosecution afterwards. They may be said to have lost all, if not more than all, they had made.

"The other partners (Henry Yates, John Ely, Jr., and James McIntyre), lately began to perceive this state of things, and it gave them pain and distress to think that the two first partners, who had been subjected to the severest losses, responsibilities, labors and anxieties, should after all be left with very little for their remuneration. What was to be done was the question with those three gentlemen who sent you the communication of which you complain.

"They were fully satisfied of the legality, as well as equity,† under the circumstances of withholding what had been cheerfully given gratuitously to a meritorious and public spirited man, for a valuable public object, so long as they entertained the opinion that necessity did not require another course. Now, however, . . .

* The present Yates & McIntyre, including Henry Yates, Jr., John Ely, Jr., and James McIntyre, attributed the losses of A. McIntyre and J. B. Yates, the original Yates & McIntyre, to a very different cause from that to which they themselves attributed it at the time of those losses, and when the cause was fresh in their memory.

In Sept. 29, 1828, they say in a letter addressed to the President—

"We are now drawing to a close with our arrangements in consequence of our foolish and temerarious speculations." (*Chancery docs.* § 151.)

And even Mr. Henry Yates assigns, again and again, the pressure of the *Welland canal drafts* as the cause of their embarrassments, never their want of experience in the lottery business, a business, in which Mr. J. B. Yates had been engaged years before this contract with Union College was entered into. (*Chancery docs.* § 138.)

† The opinion of the present Yates & McIntyre, seems to have undergone a material change in relation to the claims of honor and equity, since they applied during the continuance of their embarrassment, to the President, for one more concession, granted in the very stipulation, the payment promised in which, they now repudiate.

Then they spoke doubtfully of their own legal rights, but admitted the equitable rights of the President to be unquestionable. In relation to this, Mr. Archibald McIntyre, in a letter addressed to him, May 15th, 1830, says:

"You are aware, I believe, that although *we may* have a legal right in the lotteries drawn or to be drawn, subsequent to our first contract with you, that your right to a participation in having satisfied themselvs that the situation of the two first partners imperiously demanded what is now claimed for them, they deemed it their duty to communicate to you their intentions in the manner they did, at the same time informing the other two, (J. B. Y. and A. McI.) that they claimed no part of what yet might be saved in the way proposed, but generously offered to apply it to making up, in part, the losses sustained in the early part of the business.*

"With these views of this subject, we hope you will see abundant reason for concurring in the course determined in. The measure was not hastily, nor without reflection, adopted.

"We trust that you will believe us, when we assure you that it gives us great pain to think that any difference of opinion should take place with you, a man whom we so much revere and respect, and that it is now our most anxious wish, that on a full review of the matter, you will be able to see it in a very different light from that in which, by your letter, you seem to have done.

"We are, with sincere respect, Rev. Sir,

"Your most obedient servants,

YATES & McINTYRE."

"Rev. E. Nott, D. D." (*Chan. Docs.* § 500 to 507.)

So much as to the consistency of enquiring after payments made the President for personal services, all of which had been reported to the Trustees, and forbearing to enquire after payments made the Treasurer, none of which had been so reported, as stated page 19.

their avails, is at least questionable. But however this may be, I declare most unequivocally that I have not the remotest idea (nor do I know that any one else has) of setting up such a construction, *or of getting rid, in any way, of all that is in honor and equity yours.* We have gone on, hand in hand, and obtained extraordinary rights by dint of talent, management, prudence and perseverance; and the exertion of your talents and management, were undoubtedly most efficient in the obtainment of these rights. *Hence every principle of honor and justice requires that you should fully partake in the benefits; I certainly wish you should. Indeed, I could not, if permitted to do it, think of asking more than to participate equally with you in the benefits thus obtained.* (*Chanc. doc.* § 365.)

* The generosity of taking this five per cent. from the President, to whom it was promised to be paid, and giving it to A. McIntyre and J. B. Yates, who promised to pay it since it cost the donors nothing, was about equal to its justice.

(G.)

Documents shewing the entire falsehood of the statement that "all payments from Yates & McIntyre were called for as due to Union College," as stated page 19.

First. --What say Yates & McIntyre themselves?

"NEW-YORK, *May* 30, 1826.

Rev. Sir,—In order to bring all the lotteries of the State of New-York to a close, within the time for closing the Literature and Fever Hospital Lotteries, the Legislature have passed an act *holding out strong inducements* to the subscribers to accept of the conditions of the same, entitled "An act to enable the mayor, aldermen and commonalty of the city of Albany, to dispose of tickets in a lottery, heretofore granted, and to limit the continuance of the same," passed 13th April, 1826, under which act the subscribers have made a contract in the execution of which they hope to be able to indemnify themselves for the heavy losses they have heretofore sustained; *which contract, however, they cannot execute without your consent and co-operation, as it will require a further continuance of the heavy personal responsibilities assumed by you on our behalf.* And on condition that such consent and co-operation is granted by you, we hereby STIPULATE AND ENGAGE that, (after having drawn for the college $2,004,099 worth of tickets, reckoned at their scheme price, of actual sales, and $1,654,497 worth of actual sales, for our own benefit, as assignees of the Fever Hospital Lottery,) we will, within ninety days after the drawing of each subsequent class, after the drawing of said two sums, *deposit to your credit,* in such bank as you shall designate, SIX AND THIRTY-ONE ONE-HUNDREDTHS PERCENTUM on the gross amount of all tickets actually sold therein, together with *the interest* accruing thereon from the day of drawing."

(Signed.) YATES & McINTYRE."

(*Chancery Docs.* § 259.)

"UNION COLLEGE, *June* 10*th*, 1826.

"*Gentlemen*,—To the written propositions submitted in your letter, dated May 30th, in regard to the contract you have made under an act entitled "An act to enable the mayor, aldermen and commonalty of the city of Albany, to dispose of tickets in a lottery heretofore granted," and to limit the continuance of lotteries, passed April 13th, 1826, I hereby communicate my acceptance; and you will consider this as the evidence of my consent, and the pledge of my co-operation granted on the terms contained in the proposition submitted.

"Very respectfully, yours, &c.,

E. NOTT."

"Messrs. YATES & McINTYRE." (*Chancery Docs.* § 116.)

"And this I do the more cheerfully, as the trustees of the College are not made parties to the contract under the aforesaid act of April 13th, 1826, and will not therefore, be considered responsible for the hazard which may arise from proceedings had under it.

"Very respectfully, yours, &c.,

E. NOTT, *as President*."

"To YATES & McINTYRE." (*Chancery Docs.* § 117.)

Yates & McIntyre to E. Nott..

"Whereas, *the claim of Union College* against the subscribers, Yates & McIntyre, arising out of their contracts under the law to limit the continuance of lotteries, passed the 5th of April, 1822, *have been fully paid, or provided for by notes given August* 1, 1828, *when said contract was cancelled;* and whereas, *the stipulation of the subscribers entered into with Eliphalet Nott*, on the 30th May, 1826, under the "Act to enable the mayor, aldermen and commonalty of the city of Albany to dispose of tickets in a lottery heretofore granted, and to limit the continuance of the same," passed April 13th, 1826, *was for and in consideration of personal services rendered, or to be rendered, and hazards run on our account;* and whereas, the hazards are diminishing, while the difficulties of conducting the lotteries are increasing: therefore, in lieu of said stipulation, entered into on the 30th May, 1826, and of all the personal demands arising as aforesaid, out of services rendered and hazards run by said Nott for us, in regard to so much of the consolidated lottery as shall have been or be drawn from and after the first day of May last, the subscribers promise to pay to said Eliphalet Nott, within ninety days after the drawing of each class, drawn as aforesaid, after the first of May last, five per centum on the gross amount of tickets sold therein.

"YATES & McINTYRE."

New-York, July 15, 1830. (*Chancery Docs.* § 378.)

Though the overture for obtaining assistance was made by Yates & McIntyre during the drawing of the Literature Lottery, which was the only lottery in which Union College had any interest, *neither of these stipulations were entered into till this lottery was fully drawn, and a final settlement made with the College in relation thereto.* Under the latter stipulation, Yates & McIntyre continued to account until the 25th January, 1832, when they refused to do so any longer; in consequence of which the President filed his bill of complaint, in which, without the consent or even knowledge of the Trustees, he joined the College as plaintiff.

To this bill Yates & McIntyre filed a demurrer, assigning as a cause, "That it does not appear that the Trustees of Union College *have any interest in or title to the relief sought by the said* Bill, or any *equity* which entitles them *to any discovery from these defendants.*" In this demurrer they say:—"The consideration of the written contract of the 10th of June, 1826, formed by the overture of Yates & McIntyre, and the letters of E. Nott, if any there was, flowed exclusively from E. Nott, in his *individual capacity.* The letter containing the pledge of his co-operation, is expressly alleged in the bill to have been written by him *in his individual capacity.* The corporation was to do nothing, and to risk nothing; and consequently was to receive nothing, more than the moneys previously engaged to be paid to it. The per centage of $6\frac{31}{100}$ was not to commence until after the full amount of those moneys, and of the Fever Hospital grant should be paid, and from its commencement, it was to be deposited, not to the credit of the Treasurer, like the $8\frac{3}{4}$ per cent, nor to *the President of Union College,* like the $2\frac{1}{4}$ per cent, but to the credit of "your orator, Eliphalet Nott," in such bank as he should designate. So far, therefore, as the written agreement of the 10th of June, 1826, secures the payment of the per centage now claimed, (and it is only in this respect that it is at all material in the present suit,) it was evidently intended, and is so represented in the bill, for the *personal benefit* of E. Nott *as an individual*." (*See Yates & McIntyre's demurrer, page* 27.)

"The acts done by E. Nott, and by him and Yates & McIntyre, in reference to the moneys now in controversy, and more especially the subsequent modifications of the contract of June 10th, 1826, are all of the same character. They proceed on the assumption, that the present and absolute title to all the moneys agreed to be paid by Yates & McIntyre, as a per centage on the contingent remainder of the Consolidated Lottery, was vested, by the contract, in E. Nott, *in his individual capacity*, and that the Trustees of the College had no interest in, or control over, such per centage." (*Demurrer, page* 29.)

"The per centage of $\$6\frac{31}{107}$, is treated as one in which the College had no interest, and over which it had no control. It is to be paid partly in money deposited to the *individual credit* of E. Nott." (*Demurrer, page* 30.)

With respect to "'*E. Nott's agreement with McIntyre to accept for the future five per cent, and the paper subsequently sent by him in the execution thereof*,' the same remark as before is applicable; to which it may be added, that the agreement and letter both proceed on the assumption, that the affair to which they relate was purely a private one between Yates & McIntyre and E. Nott." (*Demurrer, page* 31.)

To all which may be added the words of Mr. McIntyre himself, which are as follows:

"I have not the remotest idea, (nor do I know that any one else has,) of setting up such a construction, or of getting rid, in any way, of all that is in honor and equity yours. We have gone on, hand in hand, and obtained extraordinary rights by dint of talent, management, prudence and perseverance; and the exertion of your talents and management, were undoubtedly most efficient in the obtainment of these rights. Hence, every principle of honor and justice requires that you should fully partake in the benefits; I certainly wish you should. Indeed I could not, if permitted to do it, think of asking more than to participate equally with you in the benefits thus obtained. (*Chancery Docs.* § 365.)

Thus far Yates & McIntyre. Much more might be added if more were necessary.

Secondly.—What say the Trustees of Union College as to their claiming all payments from Yates & McIntyre? They say:—

(Extracts from Correspondence with Hamilton College.)

To B. W. DWIGHT, Esq., *Treasurer of Hamilton College:*

Dear Sir,—In reply to your communication we beg leave to make a brief statement of facts.

The amount due to the several institutions from the Literature Lottery was $322,256.81. The President of Union College borrowed funds, and bought out all the other parties in interest. By the original indenture of Yates & McIntyre, to whom its entire interest was sold, said College was, (if paid in advance, and thus protected against loss, as the other institutions had been,) to receive $276,090.14, estimated with interest by Yates & McIntyre in a bill subsequently filed against the trustees at $393,120. In the execution of this indenture, however, they met with losses, and became reduced to the verge of ruin.

To prevent their failure, the president of Union College raised funds for them to a large amount, in consideration of which, Jan. 24th, 1826, they stipulated to vary the terms of their original indenture, so as to require the payment of eleven per cent on $4,492,208 worth of tickets, a supposed contingent residue of $456,489 worth, to remain subject to a new contract. Soon after this an act was passed authorising the mixing of the Albany land lottery with the Literature and Fever Hospital lotteries. To enable Yates & McIntyre to execute a contract under said act, they applied to Dr. Nott for his consent and co-operation, stipulating

May 31st, 1826, in consideration thereof to pay to him a certain per centage on all the subsequent classes drawn.

After the whole of the $4,948,597 worth of tickets assumed to belong to the Literature lottery, including the supposed contingent residue, had been drawn, and the drawing of the Fever Hospital lottery commenced, a settlement was effected with Yates & McIntyre, to wit: on the first of August 1828, under their original indenture, as modified by their stipulation of Jan. 24, and May 31, 1826, in which Yates & McIntyre agreed not only to pay the per centage due to the College under their original indenture on the whole amount of tickets then supposed to have belonged to the Literature lottery, but also to pay the additional amount stipulated to be paid Jan. 24, 1826, for monies advanced by the President to enable them to meet the payment of certain prizes.

Yates & McIntyre, after commencing the drawing of the Fever Hospital lottery still continuing embarrassed, applied repeatedly to Dr. Nott for pecuniary assistance to very large amounts, for which they stipulated to pay a certain per centage on the tickets thereafter to be drawn, which per centage, after being paid for some time, was ultimately refused. For the recovery of which Dr. Nott filed a bill in Chancery, in which the Trustees of Union College, without their consent, or even knowledge, were joined as plaintiffs.

To the bill filed by Dr. Nott, Yates & McIntyre demurred on the ground that the stipulation was entered into with him *after the Literature lottery was closed*, and that the same *was for personal advances, services and hazards only, in which the College had no interest, which was, indeed, the case.*

And the lottery question having been referred to the Attorney General, (see Assembly Doc., vol. 4, p. 10,) by the Legislature, he reported that the whole amount of tickets contained in the Literature lottery, in place of being $4,948,597 worth, as had been supposed, was only $3,693,800 worth, making a difference of $1,254,797 worth of tickets in the lottery, and of $138,027 in the amount of percentage to have been paid by Yates & McIntyre. Whereupon Yates & McIntyre filed a bill in Chancery for the recovery of this excess of percentage, claimed to have been paid in error.

After considering the report of the Attorney General, and perceiving if said lotteries contained only $3,693,800 worth of tickets, that there was no contingent residue when the stipulation of the 24th Jan., 1846, was entered into, and of course that the stipulation of May 31, predicated on such residue, must be invalid; a negotiation was, by advice of counsel, opened with a view to effect an amicable settlement, and thus prevent a protracted and expensive litigation, when it was found that Yates & McIntyre would, on their part, agree to cancel their entire claim against Union College for all payments made in error, provided the College would surrender to them certain evidences of debt amounting to $126,037.57, and further, that they would agree to pay $150,000 in ten years, in instalments, provided the claim against them for the payment of percentage under their stipulation entered into July 15th, 1830, with Dr. Nott, for personal advances, hazards, &c., was cancelled, and it was also found that Dr. Nott would, on his part, also agree to cancel said stipulation on said terms.

Whereupon an article of agreement was entered into between the trustees of Union College and the President, setting forth that the $150,000 to be received from Yates & McIntyre, was to be received on account of the stipulation aforesaid entered into with him for personal advances, &c., and for the recovery of which, said suit had been commenced, and that the same was to be accounted for to him on a final settlement.

After which a tripartite agreement, on the conditions above set forth, was entered into between Yates & McIntyre, the Trustees of Union College, and the President of Union College, in which the parties severally agreed, not only to discontinue the suits which had been commenced, but also to relinquish all cause of future suits, arising out of said lottery transactions.

The President of Union College, having by *great personal exertions and at great personal peril, (in which no other Trustee was found willing to participate, and which all considered in him rash and even presumptuous,)* succeeded in purchasing out the interest of the other Institutions, amounting to $95,780.62, and in sustaining the credit of Yates &

McIntyre till the entire Literature lottery was drawn, and having also succeeded in securing from said lottery, after paying all expenses, a considerable surplus to be divided between the colleges, it was felt that Union College, whose interest had been so gratuitously and greatly promoted by hazards assumed by him *in its own behalf*, would therefore come forward with an ill grace to claim *to share in the avails*, if any there should be, of hazards subsequently assumed by him *in behalf of others.* And however frequently the Trustees of Union College may have expressed their sense of the indebtedness of said college to its President for his interference as aforesaid, *still they deem it proper distinctly to state, that they have neither received, nor claim to be entitled to receive*, the compensation stipulated to be paid to the President of said college in the form of per centage for monies advanced or hazards run by him in behalf of Yates & McIntyre, after the Literature lottery closed.

In behalf of the finance committee,

Very respectfully, yours, &c.,

J. P. CUSHMAN,
A. C. PAIGE.

Schenectady, Feb. 23, 1840.

To B. W. DWIGHT, Esq., *Treasurer Hamilton College.*

So much for "*all payments being called for as due to Union College*," as asserted, page 19 and 99.

(H.)

STATE OF NEW-YORK,
No. 71,
IN SENATE, *April* 12, 1851.

REPORT

Of the Committee on Literature on the Condition of Union College.

The committee on Literature, to which was referred the reply of the Comptroller, dated February 7th, 1851, to a resolution adopted by the Senate, in relation to the condition of the funds bestowed by the State upon Union College,

REPORT:

That the Assembly of 1849 appointed a select committee under a resolution passed April 11th, 1849, in the words following, namely:

Resolved, That the committee on colleges, academies, and common schools be directed, during the recess, to examine into the financial condition of Union College, and into the situation of the various funds bestowed on said institution by the State, and the various transfers of the funds and property of said college, that said committee have power to send for persons and papers, and report to the next Legislature.

That a majority of said committee, consisting of four members, reported on the 19th day of March, 1850, (Assembly Doc. No. 146,) "that the financial condition of Union College was unsound and improper," and that the remaining member, the chairman of the committee, dissenting from the majority, presented his adverse report, dated March 23d, 1850, (Assembly Doc. 147.)

That on the 8th day of April, 1850, Union College, by Alexander Holland, its treasurer, submitted a report of six printed lines to the Legislature, in the words following, viz: (Assembly Document No. 190.)

"That no change had been made in the securities in which the avails of the grant under the act of March 30th, 1805, (required by the act to be annually reported to the Legislature,) have been invested, since the date of his report, submitted April 5th, 1849, in which report a schedule containing said securities is furnished."

All of which is respectfully submitted.

(Signed,) ALEX. HOLLAND,
Treasurer of Union College.

Schenectady, April 1, 1850.

To this report was appended a document entitled "reply of treasurer to majority report," extending throughout fourteen printed pages, and signed by him, which, accompanied by extracts from correspondence with Hamilton College, and from the reports of the majority and minority of the select committee above named, occupies seventy-two printed pages.

The committee on literature find THAT A VERY BRIEF AND IMPERFECT INSPECTION WAS MADE BY THE SELECT COMMITTEE OF 1849. The examination as set forth in appendix E, to the report of the majority, (Assembly Document No. 146,) although merely claiming to be memoranda made by A. Johnson, secretary to the committee, appears to throw considerable light upon the financial management of the College.

Although the treasurer complains that several "misstatements of facts, erroneous deductions, unfounded imputations and insinuations," have been introduced through some oversight, into the report of the majority, and regrets that the statements made therein, "should, through the errors in their own minutes, have been so confused, contradictory, and variant from the facts of the case," the memoranda referred to, appear to be a true record of testimony so far as they extend.* That a witness should contradict himself at different points of the same investigation is neither unusual nor surprising; nor is it more remarkable that conclusions drawn from such "statements" should be unsatisfactory to the parties examined.

The treasurer affirms (page 4 of Assembly Document 190,) that $17,000 more was actually paid for the purchase of the several grants made in the lotteries to other institutions, than would

* How do they thus appear, having never been read or assented to by the Treasurer.

have been paid on the principle of the usual rebate of interest, predicated on the time required for completing the lotteries as fixed by the Comptroller, but in his answer to the 24th question, (page 55, Assembly Document No. 146,) he stated under oath, that "the $12,000 granted to the New-York Historical Society was sold for $8,000 to Union College, and the other grants were discounted on the usual rule of rebate and premium." (Explained p. 12.)

At page 14 of the minority report, (Assembly Doc. 147 of 1850,) it is stated that "the bond of Yates & McIntyre, mentioned in schedule 6, had been paid at the time of said examination, and the amount except $2,000 had been deposited in New-York, to the credit of the treasurer and bearing interest." The President stated to the committee that he proposed, after giving satisfactory security, to borrow the balance so deposited, for the purpose of improving property belonging to him in New-York, known as the Stuyvesant Cove property, (see same page 14.)

The treasurer states, (Assembly Doc. No. 146, page 47,) under oath, that the bond of Yates & McIntyre, mentioned in schedule 6, with the mortgage collateral thereto, has been paid, and the moneys received therefrom with the exception of about $2,000, which had been paid for interest, debts and expenses of the college, is deposited in New-York, to the credit of the treasurer of the college, and is on interest.

In reply to question 12, (Assembly Doc. No. 146, page 53,) which is in the following words, "the $17,500 of the Yates and McIntyre, due with interest, belonging to the permanent fund of $50,000 granted by the act of April 13th, 1814, for the assistance of indigent students having been collected May 5th, 1849, how has it been invested?"

The treasurer answered—"It is not invested, but will be by bond and mortgage."

To Question 13, (of same Doc.)—"The Novelty works being the private property of Dr. Nott, for what reason has that money been employed to enable Hezekiah Bradford to make a dock there?"

The treasurer answered, "IT IS NOT EMPLOYED AT THE NOVELTY WORKS BUT ON THE LANDS, AT STUYVESANT COVE." (Refuted page 9.)

To Question 14, (of same Doc.)—Doctor Nott having stated that he is empowered by a resolution of the trustees of Union College to direct the application of funds as he may think fit, that he often uses the funds for various purposes, but that he always replaces any moneys belonging to the college which he may take, with some security; what security has he given in place of the $17,500 so employed by him, at Stuyvesant Cove as aforesaid?"

The treasurer answered—"It is not yet employed, but it is in the hands of the treasurer."

The contradiction between the replies to the last two questions, and the statement of the President in the minority report, although claimed to be an error, by the reply of the treasurer (at page 7, Assembly Doc. No. 190) only shows a discrepancy of statements, which the following letters perhaps, may assist in explaining:*

(Copy.)

UNION COLLEGE, *Schenectady, Feb.* 10, 1849.

A. McINTYRE, Esq., Albany:

Dear Sir,—During my absence to Albany yesterday, Mr. Charles Yates called at my office and left word that he hoped to be able to make the first payment within the next ten days, and requested that the accompanying statement of the account with the bond should be sent to you. For ten days we will endeavor to struggle on without the money; but I see no possible way of waiting longer; we are two quarters in arrear to the officers of the college for salaries; which is their only dependence, and for which they cannot be asked to wait longer. Besides this we have other unavoidable payments to prepare for, within that time. I mention these private matters to show more strongly than the mere general mention of the want of money, how we are situated, and to show that the money must be raised.

Very respectfully,

(Signed,) ALEX. HOLLAND.

* No such answers as are here imputed were ever read or assented to by the Treasurer. (See page 27.)

(Copy.)

UNION COLLEGE, *Schenectady*, 30*th March*, 1849.

ARCH. McINTYRE, Esq., Albany :

Dear Sir,—Owing to recent calls on the College for the payment of large sums of money, which calls were submitted to the financial committee, I have been directed by them to inform Mr. Charles Yates that they would require, within a very few days, the payment of the balance of the bond of Yates & McIntyre and others, amounting, with interest, to over $17,500.

I have written Mr. Yates to that effect, and the object of this communication to you is to say, that in the event of having to proceed to collect this amount by a course of law, the committee decline resorting to the slow process of foreclosing the collateral mortgage of J. B. Yates, and would deem it their duty to look for it to the makers of the bond, any one of whom, on payment thereof, could, if desired, have said mortgage transferred to them.

Very respectfully,

ALEX. HOLLAND, *Treasurer*.*

It appears to the committee on literature a somewhat strange application of so large a portion of the permanent fund of $50,000 granted by the Legislature for the assistance of indigent students, to employ $17,500 for the payment of professors' salaries, then two quarters in arrear.† Perhaps, however, this is only a *discrepancy* or *error* on the part of the treasurer, or one of the "unfounded imputations and insinuations" so feelingly and indignantly spurned by him in his reply to the majority report.

The report of the minority is spoken of in terms of satisfaction by the treasurer in page 16 of his reply, (Assembly Doc. No. 190.) Now it is claimed at page 21 of the minority report, that by a resolution of the board of trustees, the entire management and control of the funds of the College have for many years been placed in the hands of the finance committee, of which the President of College is the chairman; "and the President mainly is entitled to whatever credit or liable to whatever censure may attach to the management of the finances of the College." The treasurer in his reply to question 7, at page 52, Assembly Doc. 146 of 1850, answers: "In

* Mr. Yates having repeatedly neglected to meet his acceptances for monies due, the Finance Committee directed the collection of that entire debt. † Refuted page 9.

reply to that branch of the question demanding, 'does not the President use the funds of the College as his own, interchangeably as occasion arises?' He never has done so to my knowledge."

How thoroughly conversant the treasurer was with the financial management of the College funds is evident from a legal document, dated December 20th, 1836,* and purporting to be made between Howard Nott and Benjamin Nott, of the city of New-York, manufacturers and merchants, doing business under the firm of H. Nott & Co., parties of the first part; and James Brown of the firm of Brown, Brothers & Co., James Hall of the firm of James Hall & Co., and John Delafield of New-York, parties of the second part; from which instrument extracts are herein immediately after given, so far as applicable to the points of this investigation. And this instrument, among other matters, witnesseth, that whereas the said parties of the first part have been engaged for some time past in an extensive business, principally consisting of the manufacturing and sale of stoves, steam engines, and articles and machinery constructed from iron and other metals, and have now on hand a large quantity of materials in said line of business, portions whereof are in an imperfect and unfinished state, and require considerable expense, outlay, and some additions, to be rendered saleable in market, and are also possessed of other property to a considerable amount; and whereas, they have become embarrassed in their said business, and are unable to carry it on and meet their debts, liabilities, and engagements, due and owing, and which are to become due and owing, by said firm; and whereas, some of said liabilities have arisen and been incurred under circumstances which require from them full and prompt payment and satisfaction; *now this indenture witnesseth* that the said parties of the first part, in consideration of the above, and in further consideration of one dollar to them in hand paid by the said parties of the second part, at or before the ensealing and delivery of these presents, the receipt whereof is hereby acknowledged, have sold, conveyed, assigned, transferred, granted, and set over, and by these presents do sell, assign, convey, transfer, grant, and set over, unto the said parties of the second part, and the survivor of them, their heirs,

* That the Treasurer was quite as conversant as the Hon. Senator will appear from page 15.

executors, and administrators of such survivor, all their joint or partnership estate, as in said indenture further set forth; to have and to hold, take, possess, receive, and enjoy the said estate, property, and effects as therein set forth, in trust, to take possession of, recover, receive, and collect such property, and every part thereof, and to sell, convey, dispose of, and apply the same, as in the said indenture set forth. And, among other trusts, to redeem twenty-five thousand dollars in the capital stock of the Mohawk Bank at Schenectady, pledged to John Delafield, or the Phœnix Bank of the city of New-York, with the note or endorsement of Doctor Eliphalet Nott to secure the note of the parties of the first part for that sum. Also to redeem eleven thousand dollars of the capital stock of said Mohawk Bank, pledged to the Farmer's Loan and Trust Company. Also, to redeem ten thousand nine hundred dollars, or thereabouts, of the capital stock of the Farmer's Bank of Troy, pledged to Prime, Ward, King & Co., or R. M. Blatchford of New-York. The stocks above named were the property of Union College, Schenectady, except $1,000 of Mohawk Bank stock, which was the property of Alonzo Potter; and said stocks, together with the aforesaid note or guarantee, were received by the parties of the first part, and applied to their use and accommodation, and ought to be returned to the parties to whom they belong. In case the said stocks cannot be redeemed, then the parties hereto, of the second part, are to furnish or pay to the trustees of *Union College* and Alonzo Potter an equivalent in money or stock. In the fifth place, to pay a note of said firm of H. Nott & Co. for twenty thousand dollars, or thereabouts, now or formerly held by the Delaware and Hudson Canal Company, and to secure the payment of which note said company received the note of Jonas Holland, Treasurer of Union College, endorsed by Eliphalet Nott, upon payment of which said debt the said note of Jonas Holland, Treasurer of Union College, to be delivered up to him, or his successor in office, it having been used for the accommodation and benefit, and not constituting any part, of the property of H. Nott & Co. And whereas, the firm of Howard Nott & Co. made a negociation with the Phœnix Bank, or John Delafield, on or about the fifth day of December instant, for obtaining from said Delafield or said bank the sum of fifteen thousand dollars, and, as security for the payment of that amount, deposited with said Delafield notes and acceptances, the property of H. Nott & Co., to the amount of $8,000 and upwards; also, the note of Doctor Eliphalet Nott, bearing date the said fifth day of December, for $15,000; also, a bond and mortgage, executed by said Eliphalet Nott, conditioned for the payment of $10,000, which said note and bond and mortgage of Eliphalet Nott were borrowed. In the sixth place, to pay the balance of said $15,000, or as much as is chargeable upon said negociation, after the application of the said $8,000 of notes.

And whereas, Eliphalet Nott, President of Union College, has from time to time placed in the hands of H. Nott & Co., certain funds, part whereof was the property of Union College; and whereas, from the mode in which the transaction took place, there may be difficulty in tracing the specific funds of said College into our hands, the same having generally passed through the said Eliphalet Nott, and for which he is answerable to said institution; and whereas, we have this day accepted E. Nott's order upon us to pay to the trustees of Union College the amount which we owe on both accounts, to the extent of his and our indebtedness to said College, as the same shall be found on the adjustment of the accounts relative to said funds.

In trust, *seventhly*, to pay the trustees of Union College so much of the existing indebtedness of H. Nott & Co., whether the said indebtedness be to the said Eliphalet Nott, individually, or to Union College, as will pay the amount for which the said Howard Nott & Co., or Eliphalet, are found indebted to said College, for funds received from said College, or "on an adjustment of the accounts relative to said funds," and after the insertion of other clauses and provisions of trust, "signed and sealed by Howard Nott, and Benjamin Nott," and "signed, sealed and delivered in the presence of Dudley Selden," and duly acknowledged before F. R. Tillou, commissioner of deeds, on the 22d day of December, 1836.

To the minds of the committee on literature it seems not to be an "erroneous deduction" from the preceding document, that in the words of the majority report, (page 52, Assembly Doc. No. 146,) "the President of Union College did use the funds of said college as his own, INTERCHANGEABLY AS OCCASION DID ARISE."*

* The untruth of this deduction shown pages 16 and 57.

Another "discrepancy" invites attention. The treasurer's reply (Assembly Doc. of 1850, No. 190, p. 5,) contains the assertion that an item of $25,000, and another of $1,500 had been "erroneously" represented in the majority report to have been added by the treasurer as an afterthought to the amount stated by him to have been received by the college. These sums are recorded in the minutes of testimony,* and are recollected by Mr. Beekman and Doctor Button, members of the committee; and in this connection it is fitting to state that Mr. Disosway authorised the signing of his name to the report of the majority, in the following letter:

Monday, 7 *A. M.*, *March* 18, 1850.

Dear BEEKMAN—The day is too inclement for me to go to the city this morning; I regret it. If I had been well I should have visited Albany and met the committee there. It is hardly worth while for you to visit me, as you can say to the Doctor and to Mr. Johnson that you are authorised to sign for me any report that you three can agree upon. Let it be a just and righteous one. "Fiat justicia, ruat cœlum." I still hope to visit the capitol before the session terminates.

With kindest regards to yourself and your associates,

Yours, &c.,

(Copy.) GABRIEL P. DISOSWAY.

Mr. Disosway had previously interchanged views very fully with the select committee, and the report of the majority, when published, so far from exciting any regret on his part at its "discrepancies," or "unfounded insinuations" or "oversights," as suggested in the reply of the treasurer (page 5, Assembly Doc. No. 190,) has met his entire concurrence, as he now personally assures the committee on literature.

It is claimed in the reply of the treasurer that the total sum granted by the State to Union College (page 10, Assembly Doc. No. 190,) is $331,612.13, and this is the sum stated in the minority report, (page 3, Assembly Doc. No. 147,) always "*irrespective of interest.*" By several statements from the books of account of Yates & McIntyre, the managers of the lotteries, it appears that they paid in cash to Dr. Nott, the following sums:

* No such minutes of testimony were ever read to the treasurer or received his assent.

Abstract of amounts received yearly by the Trustees of Union College and Rev. E. Nott, from Yates & McIntyre.

From Mar. 31, 1823, to Mar. 31, 1824,			$74,430 40	1st year.
1824,	do	1825,	39,286 85	$113,717 25
1825,	do	1826,	122,414 27	236,131 52
1826,	do	1827,	46,436 60	282,586 00
1827,	do	1828,	105,347 78	387,915 90
1828,	do	1829,		
1829,	do	1830,	70,037 88	457,955 78
1830,	do	1831,	143,210 31	601,166 09
1831,	do	1832,	116,548 82	717,714 91
1832,	do	1833,	43,186 25	760,901 16
1833,	do	1834,	16,340 23	777,241 39
Mar. 31, 1834, to June 15, 1834,			4,216 32	
Notes given by Yates & McIntyre, and falling due up to 15th Dec., 1835,...			20,865 57	
			$802,323 28*	

Int. at 7 pr. ct.	to Mar. 31,	1825,	being 1 year,	....	$5,210 13
do	do	1826,	" 1 "	....	7,960 20
do	do	1827,	" 1 "	....	16,529 20
do	do	1828,	" 1 "	....	19,801 02
do	do	1829,	" 1 "	....	27,154 11
do	do	1830,	" 1 "	....	27,154 11
do	do	1831,	" 1 "	....	32,056 90
do	do	1832,	" 1 "	....	42,116 26
do	do	1833,	" 1 "	....	50,240 04
do	do	1834,	" 1 "	....	53,263 08
do	do	1835,	" 1 "	....	54,406 89
do	do	1851,	" 16 "	....	870,510 24
do	do	1851,	" 16 ys.9m.16 ds.		4,944 84
do	do	1851,	" 15 ys.3m.16 ds.		22,359 99
					$1,233,707 02

Mr. J. B. Yates states that the amount paid to Union College and Doctor Nott, was $837,284.13.

* For the refutation of this, see pages 9 and 39.

As in addition to this sum, derived wholly from the profits of the lotteries, Union College admits (Assembly Doc. No. 147, p. 2,) the receipt from the State alone, not from lotteries, of seventy-six thousand six hundred and twelve dollars and thirteen cents, "*irrespective of interest*," and from other sources, not lotteries, forty-one thousand six hundred thirty-seven dollars and twenty-nine cents, (Assembly Doc. No. 174, p. 16,) all *irrespective of interest*, amounting to,.................................. $920,572 64

Union College, however, assumed to pay, and has discounted at heavy rebates to other institutions, and repaid Yates & McIntyre sundry sums, amounting, (Assembly Doc. No. 147, p. 18,) without deducting the discount, to............................ 207,229 09

Leaving a balance, "*irrespective of interest*," of.... $713,343 55

According to the minority report, (Assembly Doc. No. 147, page 19,) no interest is computed on sums received or sums paid since 1820; and the report of the minority has certainly made an "erroneous deduction" in assuming that this is sufficiently accurate for the purposes of the inquiry with which the committee was charged, although there would be great difficulty in stating an interest account since that date, which should be consistent with the views of financial skill, which the minority report sets forth, and extols with so much complacency. To show how essentially the account WOULD CHANGE FRONT,* it will be sufficient to compute simple interest at 7 per cent. on the sums paid by Yates & McIntyre, as herein before stated, from the time of payment, to the present year; and there will result a sum of interest amounting to $1,233,707.02, which, added to the balance above shown to have been received by Union College and Doctor Nott, amounts to the large aggregate of one million nine hundred and forty-one thousand seventy-nine dollars and fifty-two cents. As an offset to this, the trustees exhibit (page 63, Assembly Doc. of 1850, No. 190):

* How this account, when brought to the test of truth, does change front will be seen page 44.

College buildings and grounds valued at cost,.......		$296,485 36
Library and apparatus,.................	$32,817 39	
Furniture, horses, tools, &c.,............	2,000 00	
		34,817 39
(See page 56 of last mentioned Document.)		
Fund for support of president and professors,.......		43,573 38
Fund for support of professors,....................		35,170 00
Fund for indigent students,......................		50,005 92
At the disposal of trustees,.......................		144,288 56
Total,................................		$604,350 56

Deducting this amount from the sum of $1,941,078.52, which includes simple interest upon the funds received from Yates & McIntyre alone, there is a difference to be accounted for of $1,336,-738.96. Were a strict interest account to be stated with the ordinary accuracy of pecuniary operations, THE INTEREST THEREON WOULD BE YET MORE FORMIDABLE.*

The above computation has been made without taking account of the incomes from 300 acres of real estate, or of the receipts from tuition fees, room rents, and other charges derived from students.

From this difference, however, must be deducted the moneys claimed to have been paid by the college to other institutions and to Yates & McIntyre, amounting to $207,229.09. These payments were not made for the full amounts claimed by the college as credits, because in the case of the New-York Historical Society, the discount was one-third of the whole sum granted † and in the other cases, there was a rebate of interest. But there being no dates of payment before this committee, an accurate calculation of interest becomes impossible. By a liberal estimate, however, assuming that the net payments actually made amounted to $200,000, which is improbable, and averaging the interest to have run twenty years, the aggregate would be $480,000, which being deducted from $1,336,738.96, leaves still a difference of $856,738.96.

The current expenses of Union College were, in 1850, $20,850, and they do not appear to have materially varied from that amount

* How much more formidable will be shown page 12. † For the answer, see page 12.

for a long series of years. During twelve years, from 1837 to 1848, the interest from the permanent fund was annually reported at the same amount *precisely*, viz: $13,734.20. The tuition fees varied from $8,077 to $5,804.43. The average yearly income for the twelve years was $20,578.59, as reported; while the yearly interest on the monies received from Yates & McIntyre alone, would have amounted, in 1833 to $54,406.89. The college buildings were finished as early as 1819, and then occupied, while the very first payment from Yates & McIntyre was made in 1823.

It is claimed for the trustees of Union College (page 63, Assembly Doc. 190, of 1850,) that they exhibit an investment by a summary statement there made of $604,340.56, and upon this claim that sum has been deducted as aforesaid, as principal money, but from this amount it is proper to notice that there should be again deducted for debts owing by Union College, (Assembly Doc. No. 147, page 12,) $29,675 51

Bonds and notes taken from graduates for advances made, to enable them to complete their education,...	18,366 86
Book accounts against graduates for similar advances,	25,082 47
Mohawk Bank stock, (Assembly Doc. 190 of 1850, pages 7, 8, 9, 10,) worth only 50 per cent.,..............	16,700 00
Total deduction to be made,..............	$89,824 84

which, taken from the sum claimed as invested by the trustees, leaves the whole available property, real and personal, in the keeping of the trustees of Union College, on the most liberal construction only $514,515.72.

It is fair to state that none but an experienced accountant can fully unravel the intricacies of the money transactions of Union College. Your committee are satisfied that a critically correct balance sheet would show more ASTONISHING RESULTS than those now set forth.* There is little doubt then, that after the most liberal allowance for errors, the present balance against Union College, and for which the trustees of that institution are justly accountable, is very large, thus:

* How astonishing will be seen page 44.

Received from the State, otherwise than by lotteries, (Assembly Doc. No. 147, page 2,) granted previously to 1803,		$76,612 13
Interest thereon for forty years only, on the assumption that the money was not immediately paid when granted, ...		214,513 96
		$291,126 09
RECEIVED FROM YATES & MCINTYRE,.............		802,323 28
Interest thereon as above,........................		1,233,707 02
Funds received before the State grants were made, viz:		
Schenectady patent,................	$28,357 98	
Difference on sale of old college,......	21,399 00	
Sale of old academy,................	571 89	
Original subscriptions,..............	2,707 42	
		53,046 29
Interest thereon for thirty years,................		111,397 20
		$2,491,598 88
The college is entitled to credit by,		
1st. Payments to other institutions and cash repaid Yates & McIntyre,.....	$200,000 00	
Interest for twenty years,............	480,000 00	
2d. Property of every kind now claimed to be in the possession of the trustees,......................	604,340 56	
		$1,284,340 56
		$1,207,258 32

The items making up this property valued at $604,340.56, were acquired at dates so widely spread, the latest being March 24, 1849, (an item of interest then due on investments,) and the earliest probably about 1815,* that it is impossible to make even an approximate estimate of the interest to be allowed. A fair deduction, however, for this cause, would still leave several hundred thousands of dollars unaccounted for.

By the legal document hereinbefore quoted, it appears that Doctor Nott, was largely indebted to the Trustees of Union College on account of the loans made by him as President, † out of the

* How probable will be seen page 12. † How largely will be seen page 15.

College funds to the firm of Howard Nott & Co., before the 20th day of December, 1836. The college had previously received, or Dr. Nott had received for its account, from Yates & McIntyre, $802,323.28. It is stated in the majority report, (Assembly Doc. No. 146,) Appendix C, that Union College received from Dr. Nott *without consideration*, N. Bliss' bond for $75,000, afterwards exchanged for a deed of one undivided half of the Stuyvesant Cove property, that the other undivided half thereof came into possession of the College on their paying the sum of $58,632.15, in 1838. On the 21st July, 1848, the whole Stuyvesant Cove property was conveyed by Union College to Dr. Nott for $177,587.06. Hunter's farm was purchased by the College for $104,800. Both these pieces of property (Minority Report, Assembly Doc. No. 147, page 20,) were conveyed under a resolution passed July 22, 1848, to the president to cancel any cash balances that might be due the said president on a final settlement with him, and after such conveyance, the treasurer states that a balance still remained due Dr. Nott of $41,340.57. These transfers and this indebtedness are certainly hard to understand and harder to explain in any of the ordinary modes of transacting business. The same Stuyvesant Cove property, one-half of which Dr. Nott conveyed to the college for $75,000 in 1834, cost him in 1832, only $17,500. So that he transferred to his own college within two years after its purchase for $17,500, the same property at a price of $150,000.

The trustees in July 1848, admitted an indebtedness to Dr. Nott of $323,727.63.

These transactions between the president of a college and the guardians of its property, although the treasurer appears to have regarded them as "erroneous deductions" and "unfounded imputations," appear in the judgment of the committee on literature entirely indefensible.*

To show what a proper and judicious administration of such funds as have been long under the control of the president of Union College, (for his trustees seem never to have interfered with his financial designs) it will be instructive to look at the present condition of the Smithsonian Institute at Washington. James Smithson, of England, left his entire property to the United

* How indefensible will be seen p. 14 and 47.

States of America, to found at Washington, an institution which should bear his name, and have for its object the increase and diffusion of knowledge. The trust was accepted by the United States government, and an act passed August 16, 1846, organising the "Smithsonian Institution."

The endowment consists of the original sum of $515,169.00, received September 1st, 1831, which is to remain forever as a permanent fund. The interest of this amount to 1846, when, by an act of Congress, the funds were placed in hands of the board of regents, was $242,129.00.

A very elegant edifice has been almost completed and paid for and the building committee have lately paid back a surplus to the permanent fund out of the proceeds of the interest set apart for the building, for the larger endowment of the institution.*

It is asserted in Assembly Doc. No. 190, quoting the minority report, that the property of the college, including losses, exceeds the *amounts derived from the grants by the State*, by the sum of $303,403.82.

Those amounts from the lotteries alone, irrespective of interest, have been shown to be $802,323.28, and with simple interest as stated above $2,036,030.30. After making the most liberal allowance for sums paid other institutions and repaid Yates and McIntyre, with interest thereon, as also stated, it would appear that, instead of the property exceeding the grants by the sum of $303,403.82, the college has to account for many hundred thousand dollars over and above the present property of the institution as now held, good, bad, and indifferent.†

The committee recommend that a skilful accountant be employed under the direction of the Comptroller, the Attorney General and Rev. John N. Campbell, of Albany, one of the Regents of the University, to investigate the books of the college, and of Yates & McIntyre, and to report an accurate balance sheet to the next Legislature.

It is extremely doubtful how far the trustees had power to authorize their president either to claim as his own so large a portion of the avails of the lotteries as $111,343.44, or to permit him to

* For the pertinence of this comparison and the justness of this eulogy, see page 22.

† For the answer, see page 44.

use the college funds indiscriminately as his own while chairman of the finance committee, so as to bring them in debt to their president in the large sum of $366,177.63, which had at various times been received in money or lands from Doctor Nott, without consideration, (see appendix C, page 37, treasurer's reply, Assembly Doc. 190,) while the professors' salaries were unpaid for two quarters about the same time.*

No portion of the grants of the State was made to the president of Union College individually, and all payments from Yates & McIntyre were called for as due Union College, according to the statement of Mr. Hemminway, the book-keeper of Yates & McIntyre.†

Your committee consider that the present very inadequate results from the means furnished by the State to this institution, call for legislative investigation in a thorough manner as a warning to future financial presidents of learned institutions, and for the purpose of preserving, so far as possible, what may remain of the intended benefactions of former Legislatures.

The report of the majority of the select committee of the Assembly of 1849 seems to be fully sustained by the facts of the case, and the committee on literature feel free to adopt the concluding words of that report as their own, and to say "that the financial condition of Union College is unsound and improper."‡

All of which is respectfully submitted.

JAMES W. BEEKMAN,
THOMAS B. CARROLL,
SAMUEL MILLER.

* For the reply to this, see pages 52, 18 and 57.

† For the utter falsehood of this, see page 75.

‡ For the pertinence of this deduction, see page 20.

(K.)

REPORT OF THE TREASURER.

In which so much of the several acts passed, and contracts entered into with Yates & McIntyre as relate to the lottery transactions, are presented in the order in which they took place; together with the final settlement of the College with that firm, as set forth in their sworn bill of complaint; and the final action of the trustees in view of the whole transaction.

"AN ACT INSTITUTING A LOTTERY FOR THE PROMOTION OF LITERATURE, passed April 13th, 1814.

"Whereas well regulated seminaries of learning are of immense importance to every country, and tend especially, by the diffusion of science and the promotion of morals, to defend and perpetuate the liberties of a free State; therefore,

"§ 1. *Be it enacted by the people of the State of New-York, represented in Senate and Assembly*, That there shall be raised by lottery, in successive classes, a sum equal in amount to the several appropriations made by this act, together with the simple interest accruing thereon, till the same shall be raised and paid by the managers appointed to superintend the same: *Provided however*, that this provision for the payment of interest shall not extend to interest which may accrue on either of the provisions contained in this act for more than six years from the time of passing the same.

"§ 2. *And be it be it further enacted*, That one hundred thousand dollars be appropriated, to be paid out of the avails of the said lottery in manner aforesaid, towards the completion of the edifices already commenced by the trustees of Union College, and for the erection of such other edifices as may by them be deemed requisite.

"§ 3. *And be further enacted*, That thirty thousand dollars be appropriated as aforesaid, for the purpose of paying a debt already contracted by the said trustees.

"§ 4. *And be it further enacted*, That twenty thousand dollars be appropriated as aforesaid, for the purpose of increasing the library, and also the philosophical and chemical apparatus belonging to said institution.

"§ 5. *And be it further enacted*, That the sum of fifty thousand dollars be appropriated to augment the small charity fund heretofore granted by the Legislature of this State, the same to be invested by the trustees of Union College, and the avails thereof to remain forever sacred to the relief of indigent students, while prosecuting their studies in said institution.

* * * * * * * *

"§ 8. *And be it further enacted*, That the sum of forty thousand dollars be paid to the trustees of Hamilton College, to be by them applied as the interests of said college may require.

"§ 9. *And be it further enacted*, That four thousand dollars be appropriated to the minister and trustees of the Asbury African Church, in the city of New-York, for the purpose of enabling them to discharge a debt contracted in the purchase of their church, and to establish a school under their direction.

* * * * * * * *

"§ 12. *And be it further enacted*, That thirty thousand dollars be appropriated as aforesaid, to the College of Physicians and Surgeons in the city of New-York, for the endowment of said college.

"§ 13. *And be it further enacted*, That it shall be the duty of the trustees of said colleges, to account annually to the Regents of the University, for the expenditure of the money herein appropriated for the use of said colleges, and that said Regents report the same from time to time to the Legislature.

"§ 14. *And be it further enacted*, That the person administering the government of this State, be and he is hereby authorised to appoint four managers, who are hereby empowered to form such plan for the said lottery as may appear expedient, to dispose of the tickets and to superintend the drawing of the same.

"§ 15. *And be it further enacted*, That the managers appointed as aforesaid, shall hold their appointment subject to the future pleasure of the Legislature, and that they shall have the powers and be subject to the regulations, restrictions and directions contained in the act entitled, "an act relative to the managers of lotteries," passed April 13th, 1813.

"§ 16. *And be it further enacted*, That no ticket in any class of this lottery, shall be offered for sale till the lotteries heretofore granted by the Legislature of this State shall be drawn.

"§ 17. *And be it further enacted*. That two classes of this lottery, as well as of the lotteries heretofore granted, may be drawn in each and every year, until the whole be completed."

It being understood if two classes were drawn in a year, that the managers could raise and pay the several grants made in said act, in six years, interest was granted for six years, and no more. Such however, were the losses and delays which occurred, that at the end of eight years not even the interest on said grants had been paid.

To prevent further delay and relieve the institutions from the embarrassments occasioned,

"AN ACT TO LIMIT THE CONTINUANCE OF LOTTERIES, was passed April 5th, 1822, as follows:

"§ 19. Whereas, the public institutions to which grants were made originally, in the lottery instituted April 13th, 1814, for the promotion of literature, have already suffered materially by delay in drawing the same; and whereas, it is believed, that said lottery might be managed with greater economy and less hazard, by the institutions interested in its success, than it has hitherto been, or can hereafter be, by the State; and whereas all that could be thus saved, by greater economy in the management of said lottery, would go to diminish the loss of said institutions; and whereas, by such an arrangement, the State would be relieved from the hazard of future losses; therefore,

"§ 20. *Be it enacted by the people of the State of New-York, represented in Senate and Assembly*, That it shall and may be lawful for said institutions to assume conjointly or to appoint *one of their number to assume the supervision and direction of said lottery, and from time to time to appoint such and so many managers thereof, for the conducting the same, and to make such contracts in relation to the said lottery, as to them may seem proper, and to receive the avails and hazard the losses, and be responsible for the payment of the prizes of said lottery for a limited time; in lieu of and as an equivalent for the several specific grants to them therein made; provided*, they will accept thereof for any limited time, less than the time in which the State can raise and pay said grants, at the rate moneys have been heretofore raised and paid, or can, *in the judgment of the Comptroller*, be calculated, with safety to the State, to be hereafter raised and paid; which time shall be determined by that officer, from the facts and information in his possession, and a certificate thereof filed in the office of the Secretary of this State immediately after the passing of this act.

"§ 21. *And be it further enacted*, That whenever said institutions shall have severally accepted in writing of the provisions contained in this act, in lieu of, and as an equivalent for, the grants to them severally made in said lottery, and shall each of them file such acceptance in the office of the Secretary of this State, it shall be lawful for them to assume the management thereof: provided however, *and be it further enacted, that from the time such acceptance is filed, the State shall be absolved from all responsibility to provide for any loss or losses that may occur on any future class or classes of said lottery, and also from all obligation to pay any prize ticket or prize tickets drawn therein*, out of any moneys belonging to the people of this State.

"And whereas the object of this act is not to increase the grants made to the said institutions, *but to contract with them for assuming the responsibility and running the hazard, and taking the management of the literature lottery*, and thus to place them in a situation to save in all future classes of said lottery, by more prudent contracts, and more careful management, *whatever can be saved out of that indefinite amount that is liable, on the present plan of conducting said lotterys to be raised and absorbed by the recurrence of losses and the payment of managers*; therefore,

"§ 24. *And be it enacted*, That the annual average amount of tickets, according to their scheme price, in all lotteries hereafter to be drawn under this act, during the term of years fixed by the Comptroller, shall not exceed the annual average amount of tickets, according to their scheme price, in the lotteries already drawn within this State during the five years immediately preceding the first day of January, one thousand eight hundred and twenty-two, *which amount of tickets shall be ascertained by the Comptroller, and a certificate thereof filed in the office of the Secretary of this State;* and said institutions shall furnish the Comptroller a certified copy of the amount of tickets, at their scheme price, in all classes hereafter to be drawn, that the same may be also filed in the office of the Secretary of this State; *and so soon as the whole amount of tickets, at their scheme price, authorized by this act shall have been sold and drawn, the authority herein granted to said institutions shall cease,* though the time fixed by the Comptroller, in his certificate may not have expired.

" § 25. *And be it further enacted,* That said institutions shall apply the avails of said lottery (*after deducting the expense of managing the same*) PRO RATA, *according to the provisions of the original act, in which said grants were made,* and make report thereof, annually to the Regents of the University, as said act directs.

' § 26. *And be it further enacted,* That if said institutions shall accept of the provisions of this act, then and in that case it shall be their duty to raise and pay the grant made by lottery to the Historical Society in the same proportions as the other grants are raised and paid; and in consideration thereof, the limitation of time contained in the first enacting clause of this act, shall be proportionably extended."

The foregoing act (as will be seen above § 20,) authorized the institutions or the institution who should assume the supervision of said lottery, *to appoint such managers and make such contracts* for the drawing of the same as shall be deemed proper. And it provided (§ 25.) *for the payment of the expense of the management, and required the residue of the avails only to be paid over, pro rata,* to the institutions interested. Still, as it also provided (§ 21,) that from the time such supervision was assumed, *the State should be absolved from all responsibility for the payment of any of the claims against said lottery,* none of the institutions interested could be induced to accept of the supervision and management of the same.

In this emergency, the President of Union College proposed to purchase out all the other institutions, and having done so, to run all the hazards incident to the drawing of said lottery, with no other security for indemnity against loss, or compensation for expenses and services, than the $2\frac{1}{4}$ per cent. already granted by law for that purpose ; provided the supervision and management of said lottery was committed exclusively to him.

Whereupon a resolution of the trustees was passed in the words following :

Resolved, That the treasurer of this board be authorised, by and with the consent of the president of the college, to accept, under the seal of this board, of the provisions of the act to limit the continuance of lotteries, passed April 5th, 1822. And that the said treasurer be further authorized, under the seal of this board, to assume such responsibilities, and to give and take such securities, and to make such contracts relative to the lottery instituted for the promotion of literature, or any part thereof, and to pledge or alienate such property belonging to this board, in carrying the same into effect, as *the president of the college shall approve, to whose supervision the same is hereby committed, with authority to exercise, in behalf of this institution, all those powers vesting in it by virtue of the aforesaid act to limit the continuance of lotteries.*" (*Chancery Docs.* § 2.)

In conformity to said resolution the president immediately proceeded to purchase out, in behalf of Union College, the entire interest of all the other institutions. This interest amounted to $95,770.62, (Chancery Docs. § 58.) for the whole of which he became personally responsible. He also sanctioned a contract, conveying, after said purchases, to A. McIntyre and J. B. Yates, the entire interest of Union College in said lottery for $276,090.14, which contract was in the words following :

Original Contract with A. McIntyre and J. B. Yates.

" Whereas by an act of the Legislature of this State, entitled ' an act to limit the continuance of lotteries,' passed April 5, 1822, certain powers were vested in the several public institutions interested in the lottery instituted for the promotion of literature, on their acceptance of said act : and whereas certain of said institutions have empowered the trustees of Union College to act in their behalf, in accepting and executing the provisions of said act ; and whereas the other institutions may empower the said trustees of Union College to perform in behalf of said institutions the same acts ; now therefore, in case all the requisite powers vesting in said institutions jointly, on their acceptance of the conditions of said act, shall become vested in the trustees of Union College, so as to enable them legally to act in the premises, this indenture, made the twenty-ninth day of July, in the year of our Lord one thousand eight hundred and twenty-two, between the said trustees of Union College, in their own behalf, and in behalf of the other institutions, for which they are now or may herefter be authorised to act, of the first part, and Archibald McIntyre and John B. Yates, of the second part, WITNESSETH, that the party of the first part, for and in consideration of the sum of TWO HUNDRED AND SEVENTY-SIX THOUSAND AND NINETY DOLLARS AND FOURTEEN CENTS, to them in hand paid, or secured to be paid with interest annually, and also in consideration of the covenants herein contained, doth covenant and agree to *transfer* to the party of the second part, all the right and title of the said party of the first part, in their own right, and as legally representing the aforesaid institutions, in and to the whole amount of tickets at their scheme price, authorized to be sold by virtue of the act aforesaid.

"And it is further understood and stipulated between the parties, that this contract shall not become obligatory on the party of the first part until the party of the second part shall have executed to the party of the first part, a bond with sureties to the satisfaction of the treasurer of Union College, in the penal sum of seventy thousand dollars conditioned for the true and faithful performance of the stipulations contained in this contract.

"And it is further stipulated that all the classes of said lottery *shall be drawn by or under the direction of the board of managers, or such other persons as they shall appoint or approve. The said board of managers to be appointed by the President of Union College.* In witness whereof Henry Yates, Junior, treasurer of Union College, in virtue of a resolution, hath hereunto affixed the common seal of the college, and signed his name; and the parties of the second part have affixed their seals and signed their names.

SEAL of Union College.

HENRY YATES, Jun.,
Treasurer of Union College.
ARCH'D McINTYRE,
J. B. YATES.

"Duplicate acknowledged by Archibald McIntyre and John B. Yates, in presence of WILLIAM JAMES.

"Having examined the within contract, I consent to and approve of the same. ELIPHALET NOTT.

"SUPPLEMENT.

"Whereas an agreement has this day been executed by the trustees of Union College of the first part, and Archibald McIntyre and John B. Yates of the second part: Now therefore, this agreement, made on the twenty-ninth day of July, one thousand eight hundred and twenty-two, between the aforesaid parties, Witnesseth, that it was understood and agreed between the said parties to the aforesaid agreement, to which this agreement is a supplement, and is to constitute a part as of one instrument, and it is expressly stipulated in this agreement that the said party of the second part shall pay, and *the said party of the second part do therefore covenant to pay, for supervision and management, the same per centum on each class immediately after the draw ing thereof, as has heretofore been paid to managers appointed by the State, which payment shall be made by depositing in the Mohawk Bank, or such other bank as may be designated, to the credit of the President of Union College, such per centum,* of which payment the certificate of such bank shall always be a sufficient voucher.

"And whereas events may occur that shall prevent the party of the second part from paying their note of TWO HUNDRED AND SEVENTY-SIX THOUSAND AND NINETY DOLLARS AND FOURTEEN CENTS, given as one of the considerations of this agreement, at the time the same is stipulated to be paid: It is, therefore, further agreed, that if before the end of the year eighteen hundred and twenty-three, the said party of the second part shall elect to pay said note in annual instalments of thirty-nine thousand three hundred and twelve dollars, commencing from the day the interest commenced on said note, and continue until said note shall be fully paid, said party shall be allowed to do so. In which event, said party shall immediately after the drawing of each class deposit to the credit of the treasurer of Union College for safe keeping, in the Manhattan Bank, or such other bank as may by him be designated, such part of the aforesaid annual payment as shall bear the same proportion to the whole annual payment, as the amount of tickets in said class reckoned at their scheme price, shall bear to four hundred forty-nine thousand two hundred and eighty dollars, a certificate of which deposit shall be sufficient evidence of the receipt thereof by the treasurer aforesaid, and the amount of the several receipts, shall on the last day of every year, reckoned as aforesaid, be endorsed; or if not endorsed shall have the effect of an endorsement thereof on the aforesaid note.

And it is further stipulated, that the said party of the second part *may at any time anticipate the payment of the stipulated annual payments as aforesaid, by depositing the same to the credit of the treasurer of Union College, as aforesaid,* on or before the first day of the year, commencing as aforesaid, in which such payment would otherwise be made, *in which case, a rebate in the amount shall be made equal to the amount of interest that would accrue on such payment during the whole time the same is anticipated, except six months; and though such rebatement be made in the deposit, the full sum of thirty-nine thousand three hundred and twelve dollars shall be endorsed therefor, on the aforesaid original note, at the close of the year,* reckoning as aforesaid, in which the same would otherwise have been fully deposited or if not so endorsed, the deposit shall have the effect of such endorsement.

"And it is further stipulated by the party of the second part, to sell on the first four days of sale, in each class, at the scheme price to adventurers, and to the several licensed lottery dealers in such proportions as may appear discreet, and to such amount as may be required, except that the said party of the second part may always retain one-third part of each class for their own use, and such other and larger proportions as may from time to time be consented to, either by *the President of Union College, or by the board of managers appointed as aforesaid.* In witness whereof, Henry Yates, Jr., treasurer of Union College, hath hereunto affixed the common seal of Union College, and has signed his name in virtue of a resolution; and the parties of the second part have affixed their seals and signed their names.

SEAL of Union College.

HENRY YATES, Jun.,
Treasurer of Union College.
ARCHIBALD McINTYRE,
J. B. YATES.

"Interlineations being made before execution, and all acknowledged in my presence by Archibald McIntyre and John B. Yates.
WM. JAMES.

"Having examined the above contract, I consent to and approve of the same. ELIPHALET NOTT."

The aforesaid 2¼ per cent granted by law to lottery managers, for services and expenses,* was uniformly paid by the State to the managers of the literature lottery till, the supervision and management thereof was, under the act to limit the continuance of lotteries, transferred to Union College.

This same supervision and management was by said college transferred to its President, and with that transfer this same 2¼ per cent. was, as appears, placed at his disposal, as set forth in the above contract; and this not only in consideration of his assuming personally said supervision and management, but also in consideration of his becoming personally responsible (a responsibility in which no other trustee was found willing to participate,) for the payment of $95,780.61, to other institutions, for the extinguishment of their claims against said lottery; and in consideration also, of his becoming personally liable for those other indefinite contingent claims to which he must be exposed in consequence of the State's being now absolved from all responsibility. But though this great additional responsibility was assumed by the President in assuming the supervision and management of said lottery, it appears from his report to the trustees, to have ever been his intention, after providing for expenses, services and hazards, to appropriate his entire interest in whatever remained of said per centage (usually styled

* An Act relative to the managers of Lotteries, passed April 13, 1813.
SEC. IX. "And be it further enacted that on the settlement of the accounts of the several lotteries hereafter to be drawn in this State, the Comptroller shall allow 15 per cent on the sum raised by each lottery to the said managers, in lieu of all compensation for services and expenses in conducting the drawings of the same," 15 per cent on the amount raised in a lottery, being 2¼ per cent on the amount of the tickets, at their scheme price, contained therein.

the President's fund,) to Union College, or some kindred institution connected therewith, as well as his interest in $8,500 drawn to a lottery ticket, which though private property he had long since caused to be placed without consideration in the hands of the treasurer.

Under this contract, Yates & McIntyre having elected to pay the sum stipulated, with interest, in ten equal annual payments continued to operate successfully till the 4th of January, when in consequence of their extensive speculations, they became exposed to bankruptcy, and applied for assistance to the President of Union College in the words following:

APPLICATION OF YATES & McINTYRE TO E. NOTT FOR ASSISTANCE.

Rev. E. NOTT, *President of Union College.*

Sir: We have stipulated, as you are aware, to pay the trustees of Union College the sum of two hundred and seventy-six thousand dollars, within ten years, with interest, annually, for and in consideration of their transferring to us their rights in the grants made by the act to limit the continuance of lotteries. It has become necessary that we should inform you, that such have been our losses that we have no reasonable prospect of being able to pay the sum stipulated, or even to pay the prizes in the lottery now pending, unless we can procure immediate pecuniary assistance to a large amount. If such assistance can be procured, we are confident that we shall be able to fulfill our contract with the college and save ourselves harmless.

"In view of these circumstances, we have thought it our duty to propose that YOU AND THE TREASURER SHOULD RAISE FOR OUR IMMEDIATE RELIEF ONE HUNDRED THOUSAND DOLLARS, TOGETHER WITH SUCH FURTHER SUM AS MAY BE NECESSARY TO SUSTAIN OUR CREDIT, until we can be fully relieved, by converting our property into money, and collecting the amounts due us, which are still good, but merely delayed in consequence of the general pressure. And in consideration thereof we are WILLING TO STIPULATE TO PAY YOU SUCH ADDITIONAL SUM AS SHALL, TOGETHER WITH THE $276,000 FOR WHICH WE ADMIT WE ARE NOW HOLDEN, AMOUNT TO ELEVEN PER CENT. ON THE WHOLE AMOUNT OF TICKETS SOLD, OR TO BE SOLD BY US, UNDER SAID ACT; the same to be paid estimating the per centum on the tickets sold at their scheme price in each class, and in all the classes hitherto drawn, as well as those hereafter to be drawn, under said act, immediately after the drawing thereof.

"With respect, we are,

"Your obedient servt's,

"YATES & McINTYRE."

The relief solicited by Yates & McIntyre, to the extent of $100,-000, was at once provided, and a short time thereafter $40,000 more was provided by the president, (*Chancery Docs.* § 98.) togeth er with other and subsequent sums to a very large amount.

Having been thus sustained, Yates & McIntyre prosecuted successfully the drawing of the literature lottery (the only lottery in which the college was interested,) to its close. This close took place Nov. 10th, 1827, (*Chancery Docs.* § 170.) The accounts for a final settlement with the college and the president were made up by Yates & McIntyre themselves to the 1st of August, 1828, (*Chancery Docs.* § 204.) and a final settlement was effected on the 6th of December, 1828, as follows : (*Chancery Docs.* §§ 229, 230.)

SCHEDULE D.—Final Settlement with Yates & McIntyre.

[From the sworn bill of A. McIntyre and J. B. Yates.]

Dr. *Trustees of Union College.* *College Fund, ($8\frac{3}{4}$ per ct. on each scheme.)* *Cr.*

Date			Payments.	Int. at 7 per cent to 1st Aug. 1828.
1823,				
May	31	To Cash paid Henry Yates, Treasurer,	$4,450 60	$1,609 46
July	30	" do paid by A. E. Brown,	1,035 30	362 50
"	"	" do do	4,330 }	2,915 50
Aug.	2	" do paid Treasurer, $1,000—3,000,	4,000 }	
Oct.	18	" do do	9,163 00	3,069 86
Dec.	11	" do do	11,662 00	3,786 80
1824,				
Jan.	22	" do	8,330 00	2,638 53
Mar.	29	" do	14,543 50	4,417 17
July	4	" do d'ft to J. W. Francis,	5,311 00	1,514 96
Sep.	1	" do remitted H. Yates,	17,958 60	4,923 63
1825,				
Apr.	13	" do do	103,492 72	23,886 66
1826,				
May	8	" do paid H. Yates,	3,000 00	486 41
1827,				
Jan.	31	" T. Gardiner's Bond and Mort. dated,	7,000 00	735 00
		" Isaac Riggs' note, due 17th Feb.,	1,500 00	157 50
		" Archer's Bond and Mort. with int. fr. 7th Dec., 1827,	16,000 00	726 98
May	25	" Three Bonds of Coll. of Physicians and Surgeons pay't assumed by us, with int. fr. 26th Oct. 1826.	20,000 00	1,656 66
June	5	" Bond and Mort. of Rob't Richardson,	4,000 00	322 78
Aug.	4	" do do A. B. Shankland,	4,000 00	277 66
"	15	" D'ft of L. Bebee, due 17th Sep., $2,500		
		" do do " " 1,182		
		" do do " 21st " 1,200		
Sep.	6	" do do " 9th Oct., 700		
		" do do " 15th " 1,500		
		" do do " 19th " 2,000		
		" do do " 24th " 633		

Class when drawn.				$8\frac{3}{8}$ per ct. on each scheme.	Int. at 7 per cent, to 1st Aug. 1828.
1823,					
May	20	By Literature Lottery,	1 class,	$4,581 50	1,666 77
July	23	" do	2 "	8,575 00	3,014 59
"	26	" Albany,	1 "	1,065 75	374 02
Oct.	15	" Literature Lottery,	3 "	9,432 50	3,165 64
Dec.	3	" do	4 "	12,005 00	3,916 96
1824,					
Jan.	7	" do	5 "	8,575 00	2,741 14
Mar.	17	" do	6 "	14,971 25	4,582 10
June	16	" do	7 "	23,954 00	6,912 06
Aug.	18	" do	1, 1824,	14,971 25	4,142 48
Oct.	20	" do	2 "	14,971 25	3,961 97
Dec.	15	" do	3 "	14,971 25	3,801 24
1825,					
Apr.	6	" do	4 "	14,971 25	3,475 81
July	20	" do	1, 1825,	23,954 00	5,081 58
Sep.	20	" do	2 "	20,020 00	4,009 55
1826,					
Jan.	19	" do	3 "	49,665 00	8,807 26
Feb.	22	" do	1, 1826,	11,977 00	2,040 09
Apr.	5	" do	2 "	8,982 75	1,458 43
June	1	" do	3 "	14,971 25	2,270 32
July	19	" do	4 "	11,977 00	1,704 72
Aug.	30	" do	5 "	8,982 75	1,206 91
Nov.	29	" do	6 (or Con. 1, 1826,)	23,516 50	2,752 73
1827,					
Jan.	31	" New-York Consol.	2 "	11,539 50	1,213 90
May	23	" do	1, 1827,	14,271 25	1,187 67
June	12	" do	2 "	11,736 37	931 08
"	27	" do	3 "	8,484 52	648 35
July	18	" do	4 "	8,462 65	613 63

Date		Item	Amount	Principal	Interest	Date		Item	Principal	Interest
Nov.	1	" do do " 25th Nov..........	3,000			Aug.	15	" do 5 " ...	8,462 65	569 34
		" do do " 20th "	750			Sep.	5	" do 6 " ...	12,759 60	806 33
		" do do " " "	550			"	26	" do 7 " ...	10,851 75	641 46
		" do do " " "	582			Oct.	17	" do 8 " ...	10,676 75	580 59
		" do do " 15th "	1,000			Nov.	10	" do 9 " ...	18,665 94	943 67
		" do do " 20th "	700							
		" do do " 21st "	2,383							
		" do do " 25th "	800							
				19,530 00	1,025 22					
Dec.	31	" 2½ per ct. on $19,530 paid L. Bebee,................		488 55	19 93					
1823, Feb.	11	" Cash paid L. Bebee, bal. int. due 25th Dec.,........		329 53	10 69					
1827,								8¾ per ct. on $4,948,597, is	$433,002 23	$79,231 39
Oct.	15	" Bond and Mort. of John B. Yates,.................		55,000 00	3,052 81					
Dec.	31	" Our note to A. Terhune, due 14th July, 1827,.......		2,000 00	146 52			By Balance, Princip.,...........	115,877 73	
		" Balance,..		115,877 73	12,506 16			Interest,...........	21,506 16	
				$433,002 23	$79,231 39					$137,383 89

Received notes for the above Balance, according to the annexed list, which when paid, will be in full of all demands against Yates and McIntyre, arising out of their original contract with the Trustees of Union College, made on the 29th day of July, 1822, under the act to limit the continuance of Lotteries, passed April 5th, 1822; and also, out of a special stipulation by them made, to provide for the payment of prizes in the class No. 3, for 1825, of Literature Lottery, drawn 19th January, 1826, and in consideration of the personal responsibilities to be assumed by the President and Treasurer of Union College, in order to sustain the contractors in the further performance of their contracts.

(SIGNED.) ELIPHALET NOTT.

For the College Fund. Notes given—dated 1st August, 1828.

Amount		Interest to	Time	Interest	Total	Amount		Interest to	Time	Interest	Total
$5,000	with interest to	1st Feb. 1830,	18 mo's	$525	$5,525	$5,000	with interest to	1st April, 1831	32 mo's	933 33	$5,933 33
5,000	"	1 Mar. "	19 "	554 16	5,554 16	5,000	"	1 May, "	33 "	962 50	5,962 50
5,000	"	1 April, "	20 "	583 33	5,583 33	5,000	"	1 June, "	34 "	991 66	5,991 50
5,000	"	1 May, "	21 "	612 49	5,612 49	5,000	"	1 July, "	35 "	1,020 83	6,020 83
5,000	"	1 June, "	22 "	641 65	5,641 65	5,000	"	1 Aug. "	36 "	1,050	6,050
5,000	"	1 July, "	23 "	670 82	5,670 82	5,000	"	1 Sep. "	37 "	1,079 16	6,079 16
5,000	"	1 Aug. "	24 "	700	5,700	5,000	"	1 Oct. "	38 "	1,108 33	6,108 33
5,000	"	1 Sep. "	25 "	729 16	5,729 16	5,000	"	1 Nov. "	39 "	1,137 50	6,137 50
5,000	"	1 Oct. "	26 "	758 33	5,758 33	5,000	"	1 Dec. "	40 "	1,166 66	6,166 66
5,000	"	1 Nov. "	27 "	787 50	5,787 50						
5,000	"	1 Dec. "	28 "	816 67	5,816 67	$115,000					
5,000	"	1 Jan. 1831,	29 "	845 84	3,845 84	22,383 89		1 May, 1828,	45 "	5,875 80	28,259 69
5,000	"	1 Feb. "	30 "	875	5,875						
5,000	"	1 Mar. "	31 "	904 17	5,904 17	$137,383 89		Prin. and Int. to 1st Aug. 1828.		$25,329 89	$162,713 78

SCHEDULE D.—FINAL SETTLEMENT WITH YATES & McINTYRE.—(*Continued.*)

Dr. *Trustees of Union College, President's Fund.*

		Payments.	Int. to Aug. 1828.			$2\frac{1}{2}$ per ct. on Classes.	Interest.
1822, May 31	To Cash	$1,309	$473 42	1823, May 20	By Lit. Lotery, 1st Class,	$1,178 10	$428 58
July 30	To do	304 50	106 63	July 23	By do 2 "	2,205	775 18
" "	To do	2,450	857 97	" 26	By do Albany, 1 "	274 05	96 19
Oct. 18	To do	2,695	902 89	Oct. 15	By do 3 "	2,425 50	813 85
Dec. 11	To do	3,430	1,113 79	Dec. 3	By do 4 "	3,087	1,007 23
1824, Mar. 29	To do	2,450	744 11	1824, Jan. 7	By do 5 "	2,205	704 86
" "	To do	4,277 50	1,299 17	Mar. 17	By do 6 "	3,847 75	1,178 26
Sep. 1	To do	6,844	1,876 39	June 16	By do 7 "	6,159 60	1,778 59
1825, Jan. 11	To do	9,173 25	2,283 13	Aug. 18	By do 1 " for 1824,	3,849 75	1,065 17
April 13	To do	3,849 75	888 28	Oct. 20	By do 2 "	3,849 75	1,018 78
Aug. 6	To do	6,844	1,430 57	Dec. 15	By do 3 "	3,849 75	977 59
Oct. 10	To do	5,148	1,012 01	1825, April 6	By do 4 "	3,849 75	893 76
1826, Mar. 18	To do	3,079 80	510 81	July 20	By do 1 " for 1825,	6,159 60	1,306 70
June 18	To do	6,936 60	1,029 10	Sept. 20	By do 2 "	5,148	1,031 07
July 3	To do	7,000	1,018 11	1826, Jan. 19	By do 3 "	12,771	2,264 72
1827, Jan. 31	To do	5,000	525	Feb. 22	By do 1 " for 1826,	3,079 80	524 58
				April 5	By do 2 "	2,309 85	375 02
				June 1	By do 3 "	3,849 75	583 88
				July 19	By do 4 "	3,079 80	438 38
				Aug. 30	By do 5 "	2,309 85	310 32
				Nov. 20	By do 6 "	6,047 10	707 82
				1827, Jan. 31	By N. Y. Con'd 2 "	2,967 30	312 13
				May 23	By do 1 " for 1827,	3,669 75	305 39
				June 12	By do 2 "	3,017 93	239 42
				June 27	By do 3 "	2,181 74	166 62
				July 18	By do 4 "	2,176 11	157 81
				Aug. 28	By do 5 "	2,176 11	150 61
				Sep. 5	By do 6 "	3,281 04	207 34
				Sep. 26	By do 7 "	2,790 45	164 94

			Oct. 17	By dc 8 "	2,740 45	
			Nov. 10	By do 9 "	4,799 81	242
Balance, ...	70,791 40	16,071 39			$111,343 44	$20,378 48
	40,552 04	4,307 09				
	$111,343 44	$20,378 48		Balance Principa., ...	$40,552 04	
				do Interest, ...	4,307 09	
				Interest on Notes, added thereto, ...	4,321 49	
				Total amount of Notes, ...		$49,180 62

Rec'd New-York, December 6, of Yates & McIntyre, their nine several Notes of hand to me, dated 1st August, 1828 according to the annexed List thereof and amounting to forty-nine thousand one hundred and eighty 62-100 dollars which when paid will be full of this account current. ELIPHALET NOTT.

LIST OF NOTES,

Given to Dr. Nott, dated 1st of August, 1828, for the President's Fund, viz:

Principal,			Interest,	Am't Notes.
$5,000	with interest to 1st June, 1829,	10 months, ...	$291 66	$5,291 66
5,000	1 July,	11 "	320 83	5,320 83
5,000	1 Aug.	12 "	350	5,350
5,000	1 Sept.	13 "	379 16	5,379 16
5,000	1 Oct.	14 "	408 32	5,408 32
5,000	1 Nov.	15 "	437 49	5,437 49
5,000	1 Dec.	16 "	466 66	5,466 66
5,000	1 Jan. 1830,	17 "	495 82	5,495 82
4,859 13	1 Jan. 1832,	41 "	1,171 55	6,030 68
$44,859 13			$4,321 49	$49,180 62

In this settlement, the entire amount paid in behalf of Union College and the other institutions under the original contract of July 29, 1822, exclusive of interest was $276,090.14. It was as calculated by Prof. Gillespie, (p. 44,) including interest $414,367. The additional amount paid under their stipulation of January 4th, 1826, with the president, as above set forth, including interest, was $104,143.89. The total amount paid under both contracts was, as appears from receipt, $512,233.62. (*Chancery Docs.* § 229,)

This settlement was made under the assumption that the literature lottery contained $4,492,800, worth of tickets, (*Chancery Docs.* § 228*a.*) which was, however, afterwards adjudged not to be the case.

During the drawing of the literature lottery, an act having been passed for the sale of ticket in the Albany land lottery, an overture was made to Dr. Nott, in the words following: (*Chanc. Docs.* § 111.)

OVERTURE OF YATES & McINTYRE TO PAY SIX AND THIRTY-ONE ONE-HUNDREDTHS PER CENT.

NEW-YORK, *May* 30*th*, 1826.

REV. SIR: In order to bring all the lotteries of the State of New-York to a close, within the time for closing the Literature and Fever Hospital Lotteries, the Legislature have passed an act *holding out strong inducements* to the subscribers to accept of the conditions of the same, entitled "an act to enable the mayor, aldermen, and commonalty of the city of Albany, to dispose of tickets in a lottery, heretofore granted, and to limit the continuance of the same," passed 13th April, 1826, under which act the subscribers have made a contract in the execution of which they hope to be able to indemnify themselves for the heavy losses they have heretofore sustained; *which contract, however, they cannot execute without your consent and co-operation, as it will require a further continuance of the heavy personal responsibilities assumed by you on our behalf.* And on such condition that such consent and co-operation is granted by you; we hereby STIPULATE AND ENGAGE that, (after having drawn for the college $2,004,099 worth of tickets, reckoned at their scheme price, of actual sales, and $1,654,497 worth of actual sales, for our own benefit as assignees of the Fever Hostital Lottery,) we will, within ninety days after the drawing of each subsequent class, after the drawing of said two sums, *deposit to your credit,* in such bank as you shall designate, SIX AND THIRTY-ONE ONE HUNDREDTHS PER CENTUM on the gross amount of all tickets actually sold therein, together with *the interest* accruing thereon from the day of drawing.

(Signed,) "YATES & McINTYRE."

(*Chancery Docs.* § 259.)

To which the following answer was returned: (*Chancery Docs.* § 116.)

"UNION COLLEGE, *June* 10*th*, 1826.

"GENTLEMEN: To the written propositions submitted in your letter, dated May 20th, in regard to the contract you have made under an act entitled 'an act to enable the mayor, aldermen and commonalty of the city of Albany to dispose of tickets in a lottery heretofore granted,' and to limit the continuance of lotteries, passed April 13th, 1826, I hereby commmunicate my acceptance; and you will consider this as evidence of my consent, and the pledge of my co-operation granted on the terms contained in the proposition submitted.

"Very respectfuly yours, &c.,

"E. NOTT."

"Messrs. YATES & MCINTYRE."

"And this I do the more cheerfully, as the trustees of the college are not made parties to the contract under the aforesaid act of April 13th, 1826, and will not therefore be considered responsible for the hazard which may arise from proceedings had under it.

"Very respectfully yours, &c.

"E. NOTT, *as President.*"

This stipulation was modified May 31, 1829, and again modified, July 15, 1830, as follows: (*Chancery Docs.* § 378.)

STIPULATION OF YATES & MCINTYRE TO PAY FIVE PER CENT.

"Whereas, the claims of Union College against the subscribers, Yates & McIntyre, arising out of their contracts under the law to limit the continuance of lotteries, passed the 5th of April, 1822, have been fully paid, or provided for, by notes given August 1, 1828, when said contract was cancelled; and whereas, the stipulation of the subscribers entered into with Eliphalet Nott, on the 30th of May, 1826, under the "act to enable the mayor, aldermen and commonalty of the city of Albany to dispose of tickets in a lottery heretofore granted, and to limit the continuance of the same,' passed April 13th, 1826, was for and in consideration of personal services rendered, or to be rendered, and hazards run on our account; and whereas; the hazards are diminishing while the difficulty of conducting the lottery are increasing therefore, in lieu of said stipulation, entered into on the 30th of May, 1826, and of all the personal demands arising as aforesaid, out of the services rendered and hazards run by said Nott for us, in regard to so much of the consolidated lottery as shall have been or be drawn after the first day of May last, the subscribers promise to pay to said Eliphalet Nott, within ninety days after the drawing of each class, drawn as aforesaid, after the first of May last, five per centum on the gross amount of tickets sold therein.

"YATES & MCINTYRE.

"*New-York, July,* 15, 1830."

Though the overture for obtaining assistance was made by Yates & McIntyre during the drawing of the literature lottery, in which alone Union College had any interest, neither of these stipulations were entered into till this lottery was fully drawn, and a final settlement made with the college in relation thereto. Under this latter stipulation, Yates & McIntyre continued to account until the 26th of January, 1832, when they refused to do so any longer; in consequence of which the president filed his bill of complaint, in which, without the consent or even knowledge of the trustees, he joined the College as plaintiff.

To THIS BILL YATES & MCINTYRE FILED A DEMURRER, assigning as a cause, "That it does not appear that the trustees of Union College have any interest in or title to the relief sought by the said bill, or any equity which entitles them to any discovery from these defendents." In this demurrer they say, "The consideration of the written contract of the 10th of June, 1826, formed by the overture of Yates & McIntyre, and the letters of E. Nott, if any there was, flowed exclusively from E. Nott, in his *individual capacity*. The letter containing the pledge of his co-operation was written by him in his *individual capacity*. The corporation was to do nothing, and to risk nothing; and consequently was to receive nothing, more than the moneys previously engaged to be paid to it. The per centage of $6\frac{31}{100}$ was not to commence until after the full amount of those moneys, and of the Fever Hospital grant should be paid, and from its commencement, it was to be deposited, not to the credit of the treasurer, like the $8\frac{3}{4}$ per cent., nor *the President of Union College*, like the $2\frac{1}{4}$ per cent, but to the credit of 'your orator, Eliphalet Nott,' in such bank as he should designate. So far, therefore, as the written agreement of the 10th, of June, 1826, secures the payment of the per centage now claimed, (and it is only in this respect that it is at all material in the present suit,) it was evidently intended, and is represented in the bill, for the *personal benefit of E. Nott as an individual.*" (*See Yates & McIntyre's demurrer, page* 27.)

"The acts done by E. Nott, and by him and Yates & McIntyre, in reference to moneys now in controversy, and more especially the subsequent modifications of the contract of June 10th, 1826, are all of the same character. They proceed on the assumption, that the present and absolute title to all the monies agreed to be paid by Yates and McIntyre, as per centage, on the contingent remainder of the consolidated lottery, was vested, by the contract, in E. Nott, *in his individual capacity*, and that the trustees of the college had no interest in, or control over, such per centage." (*Demurrer, page* 29.)

"The per centage of $\$6\frac{31}{100}$ is treated as one in which the college had no control. It is to be paid partly in money deposited to the *individual credit* of E. Nott. (*Demurrer page* 30.)

With respect to "E. Nott's argreement with McIntyre to accept for the future five per cent, and the paper subsequently sent by him in the execution thereof, the same remark as before is applicable; to which it may be added, that the agreement and letter both proceed on the assumption that the affair to which they relate was purely a private one between Yates & McIntyre and E. Nott." (*Demurrer, page* 31.)

The treasurer cannot present what followed more intelligibly to the board than by transcribing a portion of the reply of the committee appointed on the part of Union College to confer with Hamilton College on this whole subject.

"The lottery question," (as appears by their statements,) "having been referred to the Attorney-General, (see Assembly Doc., vol. 4, p. 10,) by the Legislature, he reported that the whole amount of tickets contained in the literature lottery, in place of being $4,948,597 worth, as had been supposed, was only $,3,693,800 worth, making a difference of $1,250,797 worth of tickets in lottery, and of $138,027 in the amount of per centage to have been paid by Yates & McIntyre. Whereupon Yates & McIntyre filed. a bill in Chancery for the recovery of this excess of per centage, claimed to have been paid in error.

"After considering the report of the Attorney-General, and perceiving if said lotteries contained only $3,693,800 worth of tickets, that there was no contingent residue when the stipulation of the 24th January, 1836, was entered into, and of course that the stipulation of May 31st, predicated on such residue, must be invalid; a negociation was, by advice of counsel, opened with a view to effect an amicable settlement, and thus prevent a protracted and expensive litigation, when it was found that Yates & McIntyre would on their part, agree to cancel their entire claim against Union College for all payments made in error, provided the college would surrender to them certain evidences of debt amounting to $126,037.57, and further that they would agree to pay $150,000 in ten years, in installments, provided the claim against them for the payment of per centage under their stipulation entered into July 15, 1830, with Dr. Nott, for personal advances, hazard, &c., was cancelled ; and it was also found that Dr. Nott would, on his part, also agree to cancel said stipulation on said terms.

" *Whereupon an article of agreement was entered into between the Trustees of Union College and the president, setting forth that the* $150,000 *to be received from Yates & McIntyre, was to be received on account of the stipulation aforesaid entered into with him for personal advances, &c., and for the recovery of which, said suit had been commenced, and that the same was to be accounted for to him on a final settlement.*

" After which a tripartite agreement, on the conditions above set forth was entered into between Yates & McIntyre, the trustees of Union College, and the president of Union College, in which the parties severally agreed, not only to discontinue the suits which had been commenced, but also to relinquish all cause of future suits, arising out of said lottery transactions.

" The president of Union College having by *great personal exertions and at great personal peril, (in which no other trustee was found willing to participate, and which all considered in him rash and even presumptuous,)* succeeded in sustaining the credit of Yates and McIntyre, till the entire Literature lottery was drawn, and having also succeeded in securing from said lottery, after paying all expenses, a considerable surplus to be divided between the colleges, it was felt that Union College, whose interest had been so greatly and gratuitously promoted by hazards assumed by him in its own behalf, would therefore come forward with an ill grace to claim *to share in the avails,* if any there should be, of hazards subsequently assumed by him *in behalf of others,* and however frequently the trustees of Union College may have expressed their sense of the indebtedness of said college to its president for his interference as aforesaid, still they deem it proper distinctly to state that they neither received, nor claim to be entitled to receive the compensation stipulated to be paid to the president of said college in the form of per centage for moneys, advances or hazards run by him in behalf of Yates and McIntyre."

J. P. CUSHMAN.
A. C. PAIGE.

To which may be added what follows from the report of the select committee :

" It has appeared to your committee

" That the embarrassments of Messrs. Yates and McIntyre, according to their own statements, arose from speculations entered into by them apart from the lottery business, and wholly unconnected with Union College.

" That such was the nature and extent of their embarrassments, that they would have been ruined, but for the timely and efficient and continued aid afforded them by the President of the College. That the contracts made by them with the president, were upon adequate and full consideration ; and that the frequent changes complained of by Yates & McIntyre, were in fact made at their urgent request; and that the repeated modifications have invariably been in their own favor. That the president has furnished extensive means, performed important services and run great personal hazards, for the contractors on their repeated applications, and this evidently without any sinister motive, without the design of personal gain ; but for the sole purpose of aiding the contractors, and of securing and advancing the interests of Union College, or some kindred institution connected therewith. That the course of the president throughout all the novel and difficult emergencies which have occurred in conducting this whole business, has been marked by fairness and liberality towards the contractors, and by firmness, sagacity and disinterested zeal for the interests of the college and of education. That the full powers with which he was invested by the trustees, have been exercised with wisdom and success ; and from the information they have received of his views in relation to this whole subject, your committee are of opinion that the interests of the college and of science require that these plenary powers should be continued.

" Your committee therefore recommend, that the present treasurer of Union College be authorized, by and with the advice of the financial committee, to perform hereafter, in any transactions springing out of the supervision of the lotteries, all the acts that the former treasurer was authorized to perform. That by and with the advice of the financial committee, he receive from the president any bonds and mortgages, or other property, taken by him during the supervision of said lotteries ; and co-operate with him so far as may be, in the investment and management of any funds that have been or may be hereafter received by him in consideration of personal services rendered and hazards ran; but which funds are intended for the ultimate benefit of Union College, or some kindred institution connected therewith.

"All of which is respectfully submitted,

W. L. MARCY,
SILAS WRIGHT, Jr.
JOHN P. CUSHMAN
Committee.

"All which is respectfully submitted,

ALEXANDER HOLLAND, *Treasurer.*

Schenectady, July 26th, 1852.

WHEREUPON THE FOLLOWING RESOLUTIONS WERE ADOPTED.

I. Whereas the $2\frac{1}{4}$ per cent granted by law, and uniformly paid to lottery managers for services and expenses, was by contract, placed at the disposal of the President, in consideration not only of his assuming, personally the supervision and management of the Literature Lottery, but in consideration also of his becoming personally responsible for the payment of $95,780.61 to other institutions for the extinguishment of their claims against said lottery, and in consideration also of his assuming personally, in behalf of the institution, other and greater responsibilities, as hereinbefore set forth: See p. 104 and 109.

And whereas it appears from his reports to the Trustees that it has ever been his intention, after providing for expenses, services and hazards, to appropriate to Union College or some kindred institution connected therewith, his entire interest in whatever remained of said per centage, as well as his entire interest in $8,500 heretofore drawn by a lottery ticket, which though private property, has been deposited, without consideration, in the hands of the Treasurer of this Board: See annual report to Leg: April 19th, 1823, p. 7.

"Therefore, resolved, That all amounts arising from either of the aforesaid sources, or otherwise, which have been deposited with the Treasurer, by the President, without consideration, be passed to his credit in the books of the college, and accounted for to him by the Treasurer with the assent and concurrence of the two other members of the finance committee on a final settlement, that the same may be included in the special fund instituted by him in conformity to his reports to this board, July 1831, 1832 and 1833; (see pages 32, 33, 34,) in conformity to an act of the Legislature, passed 14th May, 1840, authorizing certain trusts, and an act passed May 26, 1841, amending the same; and in conformity to the resolutions of this board, passed July 26th, 1837, and July 27, 1841. (*Book of Minutes No.* 3, *page* 122.)

II. Whereas the only stipulation ever entered into by the President of Union College with Yates & McIntyre in which the college was made jointly responsible, and therefore entitled jointly to share in the profits, if any, was that of Jan. 4, 1826, (*Chan. Doc.* §80,) p. 108, modifying the original contract with said firm, of July 29, 1822, (*Chancery Docs.* §29;) and whereas Union College has not, and never had, any interest in or control over the Fever Hospital Lottery, the Albany Land Lottery, or any other lottery drawn after the 10th Nov. 1827, when the Literature Lottery closed; (*Chancery Docs.* §170:) And whereas the above recited stipulation entered into by Yates & McIntyre, May 30, 1826, to pay to Eliphalet Nott, 6 $\frac{31}{100}$ per cent; (*Chancery Docs.* §259,) and also the above recited stipulation of July 15, 1830, substituted for that of May 30, 1826, to pay to him 5 per cent out of profits of lotteries to be subsequently drawn, were in consideration of advances made, services rendered and hazards run by him personally in their behalf, in which the college had no interest; and whereas, the said E. Nott, has nevertheless signified, in his reports as President, heretofore made to this board, that it was his intention, "after providing for expenses, services and hazards, to appropriate the residue of the avails of said stipulations to Union College, or some kindred institution connected therewith :" p. 114 and 115.

Therefore resolved, That any payments arising out of said stipulations that have been, or may hereafter be received by the Treasurer of Union College, be also credited to the President, and accounted for to him by the Treasurer, with such assent and concurrence in said final settlement, that the same may also be included in said special fund instituted by him as aforesaid, in conformity to the resolution by this Board passed July 26, 1837. p. 48.

The resolutions referred to above are as follows

" Whereas, Dr. Nott has signified to the committee his readiness to transfer to Union College, not only its entire portion of said lands, bonds and mortgages, to be held in its own right, *but also the portion belonging to himself*, on the terms heretofore set forth in his reports to this board for the years 1831 and 1832, as soon as the same shall be definitively ascertained. * * *

" And further, that the treasurer be also authorized to receive from Dr. Nott in like manner, the remaining portion of said additional amounts which shall be found to belong to him, and enter the same in a separate fund, to be denominated Dr. Nott's Fund, and to be held and applied conformably to to the aforesaid report of Dr. Nott to this board, of July, 1831, and that a separate annual report be made, hereafter, thereon to this board."

I certify the above to be a true extract from the minutes of the board of trustees of Union College, at a meeting held at Schenectady, July 26th, 1837.

Nov. 28, 1851. L. H. WILLARD, *Acting Register.*

In conformity to the above resolutions, and that the balance, when ascertained, may be carried to the special fund in question, for the use of Union College, as set forth in said report of Doctor Nott, the subjoined account has been made out as directed by the board of trustees, July 26, 1852.

Dr. *Dr. E. Nott in account for special deposits made with Treasurer of Union College.* Cr.

Date	Particulars	Interest	Amount
1819. July 8.	By cash, ...		$8,500 00
	By interest to July 22, 1845, ...	$15,493 13	
1830. Nov. 15.	By cash, ...		42,000 00
	By interest,......	37,292 72	
1834. July 2.	Stuyvesant Cove,* (mort'ge on half,)		75,225 32
	No interest.		
1837. July 27.	By cash on Yates' & McIntyre's Ely & McIntyre bond rec'd on settlem't of suit comm'ced by E. Nott, for balance due him from said firm under stipulat'n of July 1, 1830. (See stipulation, page 115,)		10,000 00
	Carried forward,	$52,785 85	$135,725 32

* See page 48.

DR. *Dr. E. Nott in account for special deposit made with Treasurer of Union College.*—(CONTINUED.) CR.

Date	Item	Interest	Amount
1837.	Bro't forward,.	$52,785 85	$135,725 32
July 27.	By interest,......	5,588 33	
Dec. 9.	By cash on bond, .		10,000 00
	By interest,......	5,333 61	
1838.			
Jan. 10.	By cash on bond, .		5,000 00
	By interest,......	2,636 67	
May 24.	By cash on bond, .		5,000 00
	By interest,......	2,506 39	
July 16.	By cash on bond, .		3,033 00
	By interest,......	1,496 71	
Nov. 1.	By cash on bond, .		5,000 00
	By interest,......	2,353 75	
" 27.	By Stuyvesant Cove (unpaid on half,) No interest.		16,367 85
1839.			
Aug. 1.	By cash on bond, .		17,557 50
	By interest, ...	7,343 36	
" 24.	By cash on bond,..		1 76
	By interest,......	70	
1840.			
Aug. 1.	By cash on bond,..		21,840 00
	By interest,......	7,605 78	
1841.			
Aug. 2.	By cash on bond,..		6,860 00

Date	Item	Amount
1845.		
July 22.	Balance carried forward,.......	$410,415 92

Date	Item	Interest	Amount
	By interest,......	1,908 45	
Nov 4.	By cash on bond,..		6,000 00
	By interest,......	1,561 00	
1842			
Aug. 3.	By cash on bond,..		6,538 24
	By interest,......	1,360 66	
Dec. 22.	By cash on bond,..		2,000 00
	By interest,......	361 67	
1843.			
Jan. 11.	By cash on bond,..		1,481 02
	By interest,......	262 35	
Mar. 1.	By cash on bond,..		1,478 71
	By interest,......	247 53	
Aug. 5.	By cash on bond,..		6,277 21
	By interest,......	862 94	
1844.			
Feb. 10.	By cash on bond,..		59,007 19
	By interest,......	5,989 23	
1845.			
May 1.	By cash on bond,..		1,025 20
	By interest,......	17 94	
	Interest on acc't,...........		100,222 92
			$410,415 92

Dr. *Dr. E. Nott in account for special deposits made with Treasurer of Union College.*—(Continued.) **Cr.**

Date	Dr.		
1846.			
June 5.	To Stuyvesant Cove,*		$150,225 42
	To int. from Nov. 27, 1838, to July 31, 1852, on $58,-632.15, ...	$53,400 85	
July 21.	To Hunter farm,..		100,000 00
	To interest from Nov. 21, 1838, to July 31, 1852,....	97,611 06	
1848.			
Sept. 21.	To cash,.........		41,340 57
	Int. to July 31, '52,	11,173 42	
	Interest on acc't,............		162,185 53

Date	Cr.		
1845.			
July 22.	By balance brought forward,....		$410,415 92
	By interest to July 31, 1852,......	$201,822 03	
" 28.	By cash on bond,..		800 00
	By interest,......	406 00	
Aug. 8.	By cash on bond,..		1,335 67
	By interest,......	652 65	
" 31.	By cash on bond,..		680 36
	By interest,......	329 40	
Dec. 31.	By cash on bond,..		733 48
	By interest,......	338 02	
1846.			
Apr. 13.	By cash on bond,..		1,261 75
	By interest,......	556 43	
1847.			
June 2.	By cash on bond,..		4,021 31
	By interest,......	1,452 81	
Nov. 1.	By cash on bond,..		3,998 70
	By interest, ...	1,329 57	
1848.			
Sept. 2.	By cash on bond,..		4,286 86
	By interest,......	1,174 49	
Nov. 1.	By Mohawk Bank stock, estimated value including		

					dividends declared,...........		25,000 00
				1849. May 5.	By cash on bond, balance in full, .		19,873 79
					By int. from Sept. 2, 1848, to July 31, 1852,......	5,353 20	
1852. July 31.	Balance carried down,.........		232,070 92		Interest on acc't,............		213,414 60
			$685,822 44				$685,822 44
				1852. July 31.	By balance brought down,.....		$232,070 92

* See page. 48.

City and County of New-York, ss:

Alexander Holland, of said city and county, being duly sworn, deposes and says, that the several amounts which the Treasurer of Union College has, by the direction of the Board of Trustees, received from the President, to be accounted for on a final settlement, and the existing balance in his favor, are, according to the best of his knowledge and belief, correctly stated in the above account.

ALEX. HOLLAND,
Treasurer.

August 19, 1852.

Sworn before me, this 20th day of August, 1852.

Wm. H. Sparks, *Com. of Deeds.*

RESOLUTIONS OF BOARD OF TRUSTEES IN RELATION TO TRUST FUNDS, *under the aforesaid acts of May* 14, 1840, (page 49,) *passed July* 21, 1840, *with special reference to the Trust Fund in contemplation from President Nott.*

Whereas, by a statute of the Legislature of this State, entitled "an act authorizing certain trusts," passed May 14, 1840; and by a statute entitled "an act in addition to the act authorizing certain trusts, passed May 14, 1840," which last mentioned statute was passed May 26, 1841, real and personal property may be granted, conveyed, devised and bequeathed to any incorporated college, or other literary incorporated institution in this State, in trust; 1. To establish and maintain an observatory; 2. To found and maintain professorships and scholarships; 3. To provide and keep in repair a place for the burial of the dead; or 4. For any other specific purposes comprehended in the general objects authorised by their respective charters; which trusts may be created subject to such conditions and visitations as may be prescribed by the grantor or donor, and agreed to by the trustees, and are to continue for such time as may be necessary to accomplish the purposes for which they were created.

And whereas, it is desirable that the terms and conditions on which the trustees of Union College will receive such grants, devises and bequests of real or personal property for the objects above specified should be known, to the end that enlightened and benevolent individuals disposed to promote any of the said objects, may feel assured that their designs will be faithfully and strictly executed, therefore,

Resolved, That this board will accept the conveyance, devise or bequest of real or personal property, in trust, for the endowment of a professorship in any of the sciences, arts or professions, provided such property shall be sufficient to produce an income of at least one thousand five hundred dollars annually, upon the following terms, conditions and stipulations:

1. The donor shall be entitled during his life to nominate to the trustees a proper person to fill such professorship, and if the same be not concurred in by them, to make other nominations until some one shall be accepted and agreed to by the said trustees; and any vacancy that may happen to be filled in like manner.

2. The donor may in the instrument creating the trust, or in any other writing signed by him, appoint a visitor or visitors to act either in his stead during his life time, or after his decease, who shall have authority, and whose duty it shall be to see that the property transferred is safely and prudently invested and managed, that its income is faithfully applied to the objects of

the trust, and that the incumbent of the professorship duly fulfills all the duties appertaining thereto.

3. The donor may provide for the appointment of such visitor or visitors as often as vacancies may happen, in such manner as he may deem expedient; but in case no such provision be made, or the same be not executed within one year after any vacancy, the trustees of Union College shall appoint such visitor or visitors with all the privileges and authority, and subject to all the duties of his predecessor.

4. The visitor or visitors, after the decease of the donor, or during his life time if authorised by him, shall be entitled to nominate an incumbent to the professorship in the same manner as herein provided in respect to the grantor.

5. All nominations of a professor shall be in writing, and shall be made within one year after the occurrence of a vacancy; and if none be made within that time, the Board of Trustees may proceed to appoint a professor without any nomination.

6. The donor may prescribe the name of the professorship: if not prescribed by him the trustees will give it the name of the donor.

Resolved, That this board will accept the conveyance, devise or bequest of real or personal property, in trust, for the endowment of scholarships in Union College, provided such property shall be sufficient to produce an income of at least one hundred and fifty dollars annually for each scholarship, upon the following conditions:

1. The donor, and such individuals or public bodies as he may designate, shall have the right to designate the persons who shall enjoy the benefit of the scholarships; such persons, however, to be subject to the ordinary discipline of the college, and to suspension and expulsion in the same manner as other pupils.

2. In case a scholarship shall be vacant for one year, in consequence of the omission of the donor or those authorised by him to designate a person to fill it, such vacancy may be supplied by the Board of Trustees.

3. The persons designated shall enjoy all the opportunities for instruction and other advantages offered by this college to its pupils, and shall receive their board in the commons provided by the trustees, free of all charges and expenses.

4. Unless otherwise directed by the donor, the scholarships shall be designated by his name.

At a meeting of the Board of Trustees held July 27, 1852, it was

Resolved, That a sum less than $25,000 will be received in trust by this Board, as a foundation of a professorship, provided it is understood that the same shall be allowed to accumulate before said professorship is filled, until principal and interest together shall amount to twenty-five thousand dollars.

Resolved, That the founder or the visitor or visitors, of funds given for the foundation of professorships, scholarships, an observatory or cemetery, shall have free access to the books in which the same are kept; and provided the founder of a professorship shall waive in his own behalf, and in behalf of the visitor or visitors appointed by him, the exclusive right of nominating the candidates for filling the professorship or professorships so founded, he, or the visitor or visitors appointed by him, shall be entitled to meet with the Board of Trustees, and to vote on all questions in relation to the filling or vacating of said professorships, or in relation to the use and management of said funds.

I certify the foregoing resolutions are correctly copied from the Records of the Board of Trustees.

LEVI WILLARD, *Register.*

RESOLUTIONS OF THE SENATE.

Resolved, That the Comptroller, the Attorney General and John N. Campbell, one of the Regents of the University, have power to employ a skillful accountant, and send for persons and papers, to examine into the pecuniary affairs of Union College, and report upon the same to the next Legislature.—(*Senate Journal* 1851, *page* 526.)

Resolved, That the commission appointed by the Senate on the 12th of April, 1851, to employ a skillful accountant to examine the pecuniary affairs of Union College, and to report upon the same, be instructed, themselves, or a majority of them, personally to visit the College, and re-examine the proceedings heretofore had in relation thereto, and to investigate and report to the next Legislature upon the following subjects connected with said College:

1. Whether the funds granted by the State to Union College have been duly applied to the objects specified in the respective grants:
2. Whether the permanent funds so granted remain entire, and are safely invested;
3. Whether any funds belonging to the College have been applied to any personal purpose by the president, or any other officer or person;
4. Whether any and what losses have occurred in the management of the College, and the causes of such losses;
5. Whether the president or any other officer has, while in the employment of the College, participated individually in the profits of any loteries which were appropriated by the acts granting such lotteries to Union College; and that the commission appointed by the resolution referred to, or a majority of them, be empowered to employ some person authorized by law to administer an oath to persons examined by such commission.

On motion of Mr. Babcock, amended by adding the following:

Resolved, That David Buel and Philip S. Van Rensselaer, two of the Regents of the University, be added to the persons appointed by the Senate on the 12th of April last, to perform certain duties in relation to the pecuniary affairs of Union College

INDEX.

A.

B.

C.

D.

F.

H.

I

L.

M.

N.

P.

R.

S.

T.

UNIVERSITY OF MICHIGAN
3 9015 03553 1683

www.ingramcontent.com/pod-product-compliance
Lightning Source LLC
LaVergne TN
LVHW021414110826
845150LV00007B/1918

* 9 7 8 1 4 2 5 5 1 0 2 6 8 *